BLACK REBELLION

BLACK REBELLION

FIVE SLAVE REVOLTS

Thomas Wentworth Higginson

Introduction by James M. McPherson

DA CAPO PRESS • NEW YORK

Library of Congress Cataloging-in-Publication Data

Higginson, Thomas Wentworth, 1823–1911.
  [Travellers and outlaws. Selections]
  Black rebellion: five slave revolts / Thomas Wentworth
Higginson; introduction by James M. McPherson.
      p.   cm.
  Previously published: New York: Arno Press, 1969.
  Black rebellion consists of the last five chapters of
"Travellers and outlaws" (Boston, 1889).
  ISBN 0-306-80867-6 (alk. paper)
  1. Slavery—United States—Insurrections, etc. 2. Slavery—
Jamaica—Insurrections, etc. 3. Slavery—Surinam—Insur-
rections, etc. 4. Maroons—Jamaica. 5. Maroons—Suri-
nam. I. Title.
E447.H53 1998
970'.00496—dc21   98-7361
                                                          CIP

First Da Capo Press edition 1998

This Da Capo Press paperback edition of *Black Rebellion*
is an unabridged republication of the edition published
in New York in 1969. *Black Rebellion* consists of the
last five chapters of *Travellers and Outlaws* (Boston,
1889); the first three chapters, having no relationship
to black history, have been eliminated.

Introduction copyright © 1969 by James M. McPherson

Published by Da Capo Press, Inc.
A Subsidiary of Plenum Publishing Corporation
233 Spring Street, New York, N.Y. 10013

Manufactured in the United States of America

INTRODUCTION

A MILITANT ABOLITIONIST, COMMANDER OF the first regiment of freed slaves to fight in the Civil War, and one of the best American essayists of the nineteenth century, Thomas Wentworth Higginson was uniquely qualified to write these five studies of slave insurrections. First published separately in the *Atlantic Monthly* in the 1850's and 1860's, reprinted between hard covers in 1889 and long since out of print, they are now made available to the modern reader in this edition. A book on slave revolts is particularly appropriate at this time of renewed controversy about the subject, and Higginson's well-researched, beautifully written essays will shed welcome light on some facets of this controversy.

There have been several schools of thought about slave insurrections. Most scholars agree that major revolts were less frequent in the United States than among slaves of Latin America and the West Indies. The "southern white" interpretation of slavery, typified by Ulrich B. Phillips's *American Negro Slavery* (1918), argued that insurrections were rare in the United States because of the benign nature of slavery. The blacks did not rebel against their condition because most of them were satisfied with it. Several "northern liberal" historians of both races, on the other hand, have asserted that while there were few large-scale slave conspiracies in the United States, there was a constant, day-to-day resistance against the system by slaves who deliberately broke or mishandled tools, stole the master's property, engaged in work slow-downs, and in other ways quietly sabotaged the efficient operation of plantation slavery. Kenneth Stampp's book, *The Peculiar Institution* (1956), is the best statement of this interpretation. In a provocative study entitled *Slavery: A Problem in American Institutional and Intellectual Life* (1959), Stanley Elkins maintained (somewhat inaccurately, it now appears) that slavery in the United States was a more repressive, dehumanized, "closed" institution than the relatively humane, personalized slavery of Latin America, and thus the North American slave was reduced to the psychologically dependent status of a child. In Latin America the slaves, because the system allowed them more opportunities to achieve manhood and independence, were able to develop the organization and leadership necessary for successful insurrections, while in the United States the infantilized level of slave personality prevented such development. Insofar as it equates repressiveness with absence of revolts, this thesis may have some validity, for as Higginson points out in his three essays on slave conspiracies in the United States, the leaders in each case were Negroes who had been allowed greater opportunities than their fellows. A quasi-freedom, it appears, created the desire for the genuine article. On the other hand, two of these three plots were betrayed to the whites by well-treated slaves.

Still another interpretation of slave insurrections has been advanced by Herbert Aptheker in several articles and books, principally in his exhaustive study, *American Negro Slave Revolts* (1943). A Marxist who believes that the restless masses are in constant rebellion against the system that oppresses them, Aptheker argues that there were a great many more slave revolts or conspiracies in the United States than contemporaries or historians have been willing to admit. Aptheker's studies are valuable, but he has a tendency to push his evidence too far, to magnify rumors into conspiracies, and to elevate vague, half-

formed plots into full-scale revolts. His interpretation has been adopted by black militants
searching for a usable past.

Higginson's essays do not fit precisely into
any of the above historiographical categories;
this book is primarily a narrative rather than
interpretive account of five slave insurrections
or conspiracies, two of them in Latin America.
But as an abolitionist, Higginson's sympathies
clearly lay with the slaves. The furious energy
of the Jamaica rebels, he wrote, demonstrated
that the Negroes were not "naturally an idle
race"; indeed, their successful resistance for
generations against larger British armies proved
them "one of the heroic races of the world."
Higginson admitted that the Maroons of
Surinam committed atrocities against whites,
but in doing so they were only retaliating for
the greater atrocities of slaveowners. Black
men "who had seen their brothers and sisters
flogged, burned, mutilated, hanged on iron
hooks, broken on the wheel, and had been all
the while solemnly assured that this was paternal government, could only repay the paternalism in the same fashion, when they had
the power." Slavery itself was an atrocity,
declared Higginson, and added dryly: "If it be

the normal tendency of bondage to produce saints like Uncle Tom, let us all offer ourselves at auction immediately." The Surinam rebels had their own high code of honor; not a single one "ever turned traitor or informer, ever flinched in battle or under torture, ever violated a treaty or even a private promise."

In the United States, whites reacted with panic and counter-terror to the discovery of Gabriel's conspiracy and the Denmark Vesey plot, and responded with savage violence to the Nat Turner revolt. Turner's men slew fifty-five white men, women, and children; white vigilantes roamed the countryside for weeks afterward killing uncounted numbers of innocent Negroes, mounting perhaps into the hundreds, in addition to the seventeen rebels officially hanged. Not a single white was killed by the Gabriel and Vesey conspiracies, yet more than seventy blacks were executed for their part in these plots. The slaveowners resorted to elaborate theories to explain the existence of conspiracies among their happy slaves; it never seemed to occur to them, wrote Higginson, "that these people rebelled simply because they were slaves, and wished to be free."

Higginson was a superb stylist; his narratives

of slave rebellions are the most readable in print. In some ways his essays on the Maroons (a word of uncertain origin describing escaped slaves in the West Indies and South America who lived an independent existence for generations in mountains or forests) of Jamaica and Surinam are the most fascinating parts of this book. The exotic jungle settings, the independence of black warrior societies, the strikingly modern nature of their guerrilla tactics, and the frustration of white efforts to conquer these people have a greater impact on the reader than the more familiar and less spectacular slave conspiracies in the United States.

Higginson based his essays on research in the best available primary sources: official reports, diaries, memoirs, and newspapers. Subsequent scholarship has added some details and cleared up a few questions, but has not superseded the essential facts presented in this volume. The modern reader might wish that Higginson had anticipated some of the current speculations about the problem of why slave revolts were more frequent and successful in Latin America than in the United States. But his essays on the Maroons of Jamaica and Surinam supply the raw material for answers

to this question. The racial balance in Surinam
was 4,000 whites to 80,000 blacks, and the
proportions were similar in some other Latin
American and Caribbean societies. In the
southern United States, whites outnumbered
slaves by two to one. In the West Indies and
South America, trackless forests and swamps
or uncharted mountains were easily accessible
to escaped slaves, who could live there for
years unmolested by whites, periodically raid-
ing the lowland plantations for food and plunder. In the United States, most mountain and
forest areas were either remote from the slave
plantations or were already occupied by whites.
When swamps or forests were available, escaped slaves used them. Many blacks fled to
the swamps of Florida; some of them intermar-
ried with Seminole Indians and lived an American version of the Maroon existence. The
Seminoles and Negroes carried on a war with
the United States Army from 1815 to 1842.
Other fugitives lived in the Great Dismal
Swamp of Virginia; Nat Turner himself intended to lead his rebel band into the Swamp.

In some respects Higginson's accounts of the
Vesey and Turner conspiracies throw light on
points disputed by modern scholarship. In a

recent book, *Slavery in the Cities* (1964), Richard Wade has questioned whether the Vesey conspiracy really existed as a serious plan for an uprising. Wade believes that the "conspiracy" was actually a melange of indefinite hopes and half-formed plots among a few blacks plus rumors and panic among Charleston whites. The white power structure, inflamed by fear and desirous of an excuse to impose harsher restrictions on free Negroes and slaves, created most of the evidence for the "Vesey Plot." Higginson's essay makes it clear that wild rumors circulated in Charleston after the arrest of Vesey and his coadjutors, but it also assumes the existence of a definite and well-planned conspiracy to kill the whites and take over the city. Higginson's account, though perhaps exaggerated, is probably closer to the truth than Wade's; two modern studies, one on the Vesey conspiracy itself (John Lofton, *Insurrection in South Carolina* [1964]) and the other on the slavery controversy in South Carolina (William W. Freehling, *Prelude to Civil War* [1966], especially pp. 53–61), present convincing evidence of the existence of a conspiracy.

The Nat Turner revolt was the subject of

William Styron's best-selling Pulitzer Prize
novel, *The Confessions of Nat Turner* (1967),
a book that has aroused considerable controversy and is the target of sharp attack by black
militants (see John Henrik Clarke, ed., *William Styron's Nat Turner: Ten Black Writers
Respond* [1968]). The most controversial feature of the novel is its portrayal of Turner as
a celibate whose sexual drives were sublimated
into a religious fanaticism that inspired his
revolt. These were deflected platonically toward
a white girl whom he loved but who was the
only white person Turner killed with his own
hands during the uprising. Angry Negro critics
have charged that Styron has perpetuated the
racist stereotype of black men lusting after
white women. The charge is based on a mis-
understanding of Styron's meaning, but is given
some apparent factual basis by Higginson's
narrative. "We know that Nat Turner's young
wife was a slave," wrote Higginson. "The Virginia newspapers state that she was tortured
under the lash, after her husband's execution,
to make her produce his papers." If the Virginia newspapers on which Higginson based
this statement were correct, the virginal asceti-
cism that drove Styron's Nat Turner to commit

his historic deed was a creation of the novelist's imagination. On the other hand, Higginson's essay backs up Styron's description of slaves at one plantation firing on Turner's men while defending the master's family from attack. This incident, though labeled "false" and "impossible" by Styron's critics who assume that all slaves seethed with rebellious hatred against their white oppressors, appears from Higginson's account to have actually occurred.

Black Rebellion is good reading. It tells five absorbing true stories. It helps us to understand the nature of slave revolts. It is an indispensable source for anyone who is interested in the subject.

James M. McPherson
DEPARTMENT OF HISTORY
PRINCETON UNIVERSITY

NOTE

THE author would express his thanks to the proprietors and editors of the *Atlantic Monthly*, *Harper's Magazine*, and the *Century*, for their permission to reprint such portions of this volume as were originally published in those periodicals.

CAMBRIDGE, MASS.

CONTENTS

THE MAROONS OF JAMAICA

THE Maroons! it was a word of peril once; and terror spread along the skirts of the blue mountains of Jamaica when some fresh foray of those unconquered guerrillas swept down upon the outlying plantations, startled the Assembly from its order, Gen. Williamson from his billiards, and Lord Balcarres from his diplomatic ease, — endangering, according to the official statement, " public credit," " civil rights," and " the prosperity, if not the very existence, of the country," until they were " persuaded to make peace " at last. They were the Circassians of the New World, but they were black, instead of white ; and as the Circassians refused to be transferred from the Sultan to the Czar, so the Maroons refused to be transferred from Spanish dominion to English, and thus their revolt began.

The difference is, that while the white mountaineers numbered four hundred thousand, and only defied Nicholas, the black mountaineers numbered less than two thousand, and defied Cromwell ; and while the Circassians, after years of revolt, were at last subdued, the Maroons, on the other hand, who rebelled in 1655, were never conquered, but only made a compromise of allegiance, and exist as a separate race to-day.

When Admirals Penn and Venables landed in Jamaica, in 1655, there was not a remnant left of the sixty thousand natives whom the Spaniards had found there a century and a half before. Their pitiful tale is told only by those caves, still known among the mountains, where thousands of human skeletons strew the ground. In their place dwelt two foreign races, — an effeminate, ignorant, indolent white community of fifteen hundred, with a black slave population quite as large and infinitely more hardy and energetic. The Spaniards were readily subdued by the English : the negroes remained unsubdued. The slaveholders were banished from the island: the slaves only exiled themselves to the mountains; thence the English could not dislodge them, nor the buccaneers whom the English employed. And when Jamaica subsided into a British colony, and peace was made with Spain, and the children of Cromwell's Puritan soldiers were beginning to grow rich by importing slaves for Roman-Catholic Spaniards, the Maroons still held their own wild empire in the mountains, and, being sturdy heathens every one, practised Obeah rites in approved pagan fashion.

The word Maroon is derived, according to one etymology, from the Spanish word *Marrano*, a wild boar, — these fugitives being all boar-hunters; according to another, from *Marony*, a river separating French and Dutch Guiana, where a colony of them dwelt and still dwells; and by another still, from *Cimarron*, a word meaning untamable, and used alike for apes and runaway slaves. But whether these rebel marauders were regarded as monkeys or men, they made themselves equally

formidable. As early as 1663, the Governor
and Council of Jamaica offered to each Maroon,
who should surrender, his freedom and twenty
acres of land; but not one accepted the terms.
During forty years, forty-four Acts of Assembly were passed in respect to them, and at
least a quarter of a million pounds sterling
were expended in the warfare against them.
In 1733, the force employed in this service
consisted of two regiments of regular troops,
and the whole militia of the island; but the
Assembly said that "the Maroons had within
a few years greatly increased, notwithstand-
ing all the measures that had been concerted
for their suppression," "to the great terror
of his Majesty's subjects," and "to the man-
ifest weakening and preventing the further
increase of strength and inhabitants of the
island."

The special affair in progress, at the time
of these statements, was called Cudjoe's War.
Cudjoe was a gentleman of extreme brevity
and blackness, whose full-length portrait can
hardly be said to adorn Dallas's History of

the Maroons; but he was as formidable a
guerrilla as Marion. Under his leadership,
the various bodies of fugitives were consol-
idated into one force, and thoroughly organized. Cudjoe, like Schamyl, was religious
as well as military head of his people; by
Obeah influence he established a thorough
freemasonry among both slaves and insurgents; no party could be sent forth by the
government, but he knew it in time to lay
an ambush, or descend with fire and sword
on the region left unprotected. He was thus
always supplied with arms and ammunition;
and as his men were perfect marksmen, never
wasted a shot, and never risked a battle, his
forces naturally increased, while those of his
opponents were decimated. His men were
never captured, and never took a prisoner;
it was impossible to tell when they were defeated; in dealing with them, as Pelissier
said of the Arabs, " peace was not purchased
by victory;" and the only men who could
obtain the slightest advantage against them
were the imported Mosquito Indians, or the

" Black Shot," a company of Government negroes. For nine full years this particular
war continued unchecked, Gen. Williamson
ruling Jamaica by day and Cudjoe by night.

The rebels had every topographical advantage, for they held possession of the " Cock-
pits." Those highlands are furrowed through
and through, as by an earthquake, with a series
of gaps or ravines, resembling the California
cañons, or those similar fissures in various parts
of the Atlantic States, known to local fame
either poetically as ice-glens, or symbolically
as purgatories. These Jamaica chasms vary
from two hundred yards to a mile in length ;
the rocky walls are fifty or a hundred feet high,
and often absolutely inaccessible, while the
passes at each end admit but one man at a time.
They are thickly wooded, wherever trees can
grow ; water flows within them ; and they often
communicate with one another, forming a series
of traps for an invading force. Tired and
thirsty with climbing, the weary soldiers toil
on, in single file, without seeing or hearing an
enemy , up the steep and winding path they

traverse one "cockpit," then enter another.
Suddenly a shot is fired from the dense and
sloping forest on the right, then another and
another, each dropping its man; the startled
troops face hastily in that direction, when a
more murderous volley is poured from the other
side: the heights above flash with musketry,
while the precipitous path by which they came
seems to close in fire behind them. By the time
the troops have formed in some attempt at military order, the woods around them are empty,
and their agile and noiseless foes have settled
themselves into ambush again, farther up the
defile, ready for a second attack, if needed. But
one is usually sufficient; disordered, exhausted,
bearing their wounded with them, the soldiers
retreat in panic, if permitted to escape at all,
and carry fresh dismay to the barracks, the
plantations, and the Government House.

It is not strange, then, that high military
authorities, at that period, should have pronounced the subjugation of the Maroons a thing
more difficult than to obtain a victory over any
army in Europe. Moreover, these people were

fighting for their liberty, with which aim no form of warfare seemed to them unjustifiable; and the description given by Lafayette of the American Revolution was true of this one, — " the grandest of causes, won by contests of sentinels and outposts." The utmost hope of a British officer, ordered against the Maroons, was to lay waste a provision-ground, or cut them off from water. But there was little satisfaction in this: the wild-pine leaves and the grapevine-withes supplied the rebels with water; and their plantation-grounds were the wild pineapple and the plantain-groves, and the forests, where the wild boars harbored, and the ringdoves were as easily shot as if they were militiamen. Nothing but sheer weariness of fighting seems to have brought about a truce at last, and then a treaty, between those high contracting parties, Cudjoe and Gen. Williamson.

But how to execute a treaty between these wild Children of the Mist and respectable diplomatic Englishmen? To establish any official relations without the medium of a preliminary bullet, required some ingenuity of

manœuvring. Cudjoe was willing, but incon-
veniently cautious: he would not come half-
way to meet any one; nothing would content
him but an interview in his own chosen cockpit.
So he selected one of the most difficult passes,
posting in the forests a series of outlying
parties, to signal with their horns, one by one,
the approach of the plenipotentiaries, and then
to retire on the main body. Through this line
of dangerous sentinels, therefore, Col. Guthrie
and his handful of men bravely advanced; horn
after horn they heard sounded, but there was
no other human noise in the woods, and they
had advanced till they saw the smoke of the
Maroon huts before they caught a glimpse of a
human form.

A conversation was at last opened with the
invisible rebels. On their promise of safety,
Dr. Russell advanced alone to treat with them;
then several Maroons appeared, and finally
Cudjoe himself. The formidable chief was not
highly military in appearance, being short, fat,
humpbacked, dressed in a tattered blue coat
without skirts or sleeves, and an old felt hat

without a rim. But if he had blazed with
regimental scarlet, he could not have been
treated with more distinguished consideration;
indeed, in that case, "the exchange of hats"
with which Dr. Russell finally volunteered, in
Maroon fashion, to ratify negotiations, might
have been a less severe test of good fellowship.
This fine stroke of diplomacy had its effect,
however; the rebel captains agreed to a formal
interview with Col. Guthrie and Capt. Sadler,
and a treaty was at last executed with all due
solemnity, under a large cotton-tree at the
entrance of Guthrie's Defile. This treaty recognized the military rank of "Capt. Cudjoe,"
"Capt. Accompong," and the rest; gave assurance that the Maroons should be "forever hereafter in a perfect state of freedom and liberty;"
ceded to them fifteen hundred acres of land;
and stipulated only that they should keep the
peace, should harbor no fugitive from justice
or from slavery, and should allow two white
commissioners to remain among them, simply
to represent the British Government.

During the following year a separate treaty

was made with another large body of insurgents, called the Windward Maroons. This
was not effected, however, until after an unsuccessful military attempt, in which the mountaineers gained a signal triumph. By artful
devices, — a few fires left burning with old
women to watch them, — a few provision-
grounds exposed by clearing away the bushes,
— they lured the troops far up among the
mountains, and then surprised them by an
ambush. The militia all fled, and the regulars
took refuge under a large cliff in a stream,
where they remained four hours up to their
waists in water, until finally they forded the
river, under full fire, with terrible loss. Three
months after this, however, the Maroons consented to an amicable interview, exchanging
hostages first. The position of the white
hostage, at least, was not the most agreeable;
he complained that he was beset by the women
and children with indignant cries of " Buckra,
Buckra," while the little boys pointed their
fingers at him as if stabbing him, and that with
evident relish. However, Capt. Quao, like

Capt. Cudjoe, made a treaty at last; and hats were interchanged, instead of hostages.

Independence being thus won and acknowledged, there was a suspension of hostilities for some years. Among the wild mountains of Jamaica, the Maroons dwelt in a savage freedom. So healthful and beautiful was the situation of their chief town, that the English Government has erected barracks there of late years, as being the most salubrious situation on the island. They breathed an air ten degrees cooler than that inhaled by the white population below; and they lived on a daintier diet, so that the English epicures used to go up among them for good living. The mountaineers caught the strange land-crabs, plodding in companies of millions their sidelong path from mountain to ocean, and from ocean to mountain again. They hunted the wild boars, and prepared the flesh by salting and smoking it in layers of aromatic leaves, the delicious "jerked hog" of buccaneer annals. They reared cattle and poultry, cultivated corn and yams, plantains and cocoas, guavas, and papaws and

mameys, and avocados, and all luxurious West-
Indian fruits; the very weeds of their orchards
had tropical luxuriance in their fragrance and
in their names; and from the doors of their
little thatched huts they looked across these
gardens of delight to the magnificent lowland
forests, and over those again to the faint line of
far-off beach, the fainter ocean-horizon, and the
illimitable sky.

They had senses like those of American
Indians; tracked each other by the smell of the
smoke of fires in the air, and called to each
other by horns, using a special note to designate
each of their comrades, and distinguishing it
beyond the range of ordinary hearing. They
spoke English diluted with Spanish and African
words, and practised Obeah rites quite undi-
luted with Christianity. Of course they asso-
ciated largely with the slaves, without any very
precise regard to treaty stipulations; sometimes
brought in fugitives, and sometimes concealed
them; left their towns and settled on the planters' lands when they preferred them : but were
quite orderly and luxuriously happy. During

the formidable insurrection of the Koromantyn
slaves, in 1760, they played a dubious part.
When left to go on their own way, they did
something towards suppressing it; but when
placed under the guns of the troops, and ordered
to fire on those of their own color, they threw
themselves on the ground without discharging
a shot.   Nevertheless, they gradually came up
into reputable standing; they grew more and
more industrious and steady; and after they
had joined very heartily in resisting D'Estaing's
threatened invasion of the island in 1779, it
became the fashion to speak of " our faithful
and affectionate Maroons."

In 1795, their position was as follows: Their
numbers had not materially increased, for many
had strayed off and settled on the outskirts
of plantations; nor materially diminished, for
many runaway slaves had joined them; while
there were also separate settlements of fugitives, who had maintained their freedom for
twenty years.   The white superintendents had
lived with the Maroons in perfect harmony,
without the slightest official authority, but with

a great deal of actual influence. But there was an "irrepressible conflict" behind all this apparent peace, and the slightest occasion might, at any moment, revive all the old terror. That occasion was close at hand.

Capt. Cudjoe and Capt. Accompong, and the other founders of Maroon independence, had passed away; and "Old Montagu" reigned in their stead, in Trelawney Town. Old Montagu had all the pomp and circumstance of Maroon majesty: he wore a laced red coat, and a hat superb with gold lace and plumes; none but captains could sit in his presence; he was helped first at meals, and no woman could eat beside him; he presided at councils as magnificently as at table, though with less appetite; and possessed, meanwhile, not an atom of the love or reverence of any human being. The real power lay entirely with Major James, the white superintendent, who had been brought up among the Maroons by his father (and predecessor), and who was the idol of this wild race. In an evil hour, the Government removed him, and put a certain unpopular Capt. Craskell in his place; and as there happened to be, about the same time, a great excitement concerning a hopeful pair of young Maroons, who had been seized and publicly whipped on a charge of hog-stealing, their kindred refused to allow the new superintendent to remain in the town. A few attempts at negotiation only brought them to a higher pitch of wrath, which ended in their despatching the following peculiar diplomatic note to the Earl of Balcarres: "The Maroons wishes nothing else from the country but battle, and they desires not to see Mr. Craskell up here at all. So they are waiting every moment for the above on Monday. Mr. David Schaw will see you on Sunday morning for an answer. They will wait till Monday, nine o'clock, and if they don't come up, they will come down themselves." Signed, "Col. Montagu and all the rest."

It turned out, at last, that only two or three of the Maroons were concerned in this remarkable defiance; but meanwhile it had its effect. Several ambassadors were sent among the insurgents, and were so favorably impressed by

their reception as to make up a subscription
of money for their hosts, on departing; only
the "gallant Col. Gallimore," a Jamaica Camil-
lus, gave iron instead of gold, by throwing
some bullets into the contribution-box. And it
was probably in accordance with his view of
the subject, that, when the Maroons sent
ambassadors in return, they were at once
imprisoned, most injudiciously and unjustly;
and when Old Montagu himself and thirty-seven
others, following, were seized and imprisoned
also, it is not strange that the Maroons, joined
by many slaves, were soon in open insurrection.

Martial law was instantly proclaimed throughout the island. The fighting men among the
insurgents were not, perhaps, more than five
hundred; against whom the Government could
bring nearly fifteen hundred regular troops and
several thousand militiamen. Lord Balcarres
himself took the command, and, eager to crush
the affair, promptly marched a large force up
to Trelawney Town, and was glad to march
back again as expeditiously as possible. In
his very first attack, he was miserably defeated,

and had to fly for his life, amid a perfect
panic of the troops, in which some forty or
fifty were killed, — including Col. Sandford,
commanding the regulars, and the bullet-loving
Col. Gallimore, in command of the militia, —
while not a single Maroon was even wounded,
so far as could be ascertained.

After this a good deal of bush-fighting took
place. The troops gradually got possession of
several Maroon villages, but not till every hut
had been burnt by its owner. It was in the
height of the rainy season; and, between fire
and water, the discomfort of the soldiers was
enormous. Meanwhile the Maroons hovered
close around them in the woods, heard all their
orders, picked off their sentinels, and, penetrat-
ing through their lines at night, burned houses
and destroyed plantations far below. The only
man who could cope with their peculiar tactics
was Major James, the superintendent just
removed by Government; and his services
were not employed, as he was not trusted. On
one occasion, however, he led a volunteer party
farther into the mountains than any of the

assailants had yet penetrated, guided by tracks known to himself only, and by the smell of the smoke of Maroon fires. After a very exhausting march, including a climb of a hundred and fifty feet up the face of a precipice, he brought them just within the entrance of Guthrie's Defile. "So far," said he, pointing to the entrance, " you may pursue, but no farther; no force can enter here; no white man except myself, or some soldier of the Maroon establishment, has ever gone beyond this. With the greatest difficulty I have penetrated four miles farther, and not ten Maroons have gone so far as that. There are two other ways of getting into the defile, practicable for the Maroons, but not for any one of you. In neither of them can I ascend or descend with my arms, which must be handed to me, step by step, as practised by the Maroons themselves. One of the ways lies to the eastward, and the other to the westward; and they will take care to have both guarded, if they suspect that I am with you; which, from the route you have come to-day, they will. They now see you, and if you advance fifty

paces more, they will convince you of it." At
this moment a Maroon horn sounded the notes
indicating his name; and, as he made no answer,
a voice was heard, inquiring if he were among
them. "If he is," said the voice, "let him go
back, we do not wish to hurt him; but as for
the rest of you, come on and try battle if you
choose." But the gentlemen did not choose.

In September the House of Assembly met.
Things were looking worse and worse. For
five months a handful of negroes and mulattoes
had defied the whole force of the island, and
they were defending their liberty by precisely
the same tactics through which their ancestors
had won it. Half a million pounds sterling had
been spent within this time, besides the enormous loss incurred by the withdrawal of so
many able-bodied men from their regular em-
ployments. "Cultivation was suspended," says
an eye-witness; "the courts of law had long
been shut up; and the island at large seemed
more like a garrison under the power of law-
martial, than a country of agriculture and
commerce, of civil judicature, industry, and

prosperity." Hundreds of the militia had died of fatigue, large numbers had been shot down, the most daring of the British officers had fallen ; while the insurgents had been invariably successful, and not one of them was known to have been killed. Capt. Craskell, the banished superintendent, gave it to the Assembly as his opinion, that the whole slave population of the island was in sympathy with the Maroons, and would soon be beyond control. More alarming still, there were rumors of French emissaries behind the scenes; and though these were explained away, the vague terror remained. Indeed, the lieutenant-governor announced in his message that he had satisfactory evidence that the French Convention was concerned in the revolt. A French prisoner, named Muren‧ son, had testified that the French agent at Philadelphia (Fauchet) had secretly sent a hundred and fifty emissaries to the island, and threatened to land fifteen hundred negroes. And though Murenson took it all back at last, yet the Assembly was moved to make a new offer of three hundred dollars for killing or taking a Trelawney Maroon, and a hundred and fifty dollars for killing or taking any fugitive slave who had joined them. They also voted five hundred pounds as a gratuity to the Accompong tribe of Maroons, who had thus far kept out of the insurrection; and various prizes and gratuities were also offered by the different parishes, with the same object of self-protection.

The commander-in-chief being among the killed, Col. Walpole was promoted in his stead, and brevetted as general, by way of incentive. He found a people in despair, a soldiery thoroughly intimidated, and a treasury not empty, but useless. But the new general had not served against the Maroons for nothing, and was not ashamed to go to school to his opponents. First, he waited for the dry season; then he directed all his efforts towards cutting off his opponents from water; and, most effectual move of all, he attacked each successive cockpit by dragging up a howitzer, with immense labor, and throwing in shells. Shells were a visitation not dreamed of in Maroon philosophy, and their quaint compliments to their new opponent remain on record. "Damn dat little buckra!" they said, "he cunning more dan dem toder. Dis here da new fashion for fight: him fire big ball arter you, and when big ball 'top, de damn sunting [something] fire arter you again." With which Parthian arrows of rhetoric the mountaineers retreated.

But this did not last long. The Maroons soon learned to keep out of the way of the shells, and the island relapsed into terror again. It was deliberately resolved at last, by a special council convoked for the purpose, " to persuade the rebels to make peace." But as they had not as yet shown themselves very accessible to softer influences, it was thought best to combine as many arguments as possible, and a certain Col. Quarrell had hit upon a wholly new one. His plan simply was, since men, however well disciplined, had proved powerless against Maroons, to try a Spanish fashion against them, and use dogs. The proposition was met, in some quarters, with the strongest hostility. England, it was said, had always denounced the Spaniards as brutal and dastardly for hunting down the natives of that very soil with hounds; and should England now follow the humiliating example? On the other side, there were plenty who eagerly quoted all known instances of zoölogical warfare: all Oriental nations, for instance, used elephants in war, and, no doubt, would gladly use lions and tigers also, but for their extreme carnivorousness, and their painful indifference to the distinction between friend and foe; why not, then, use these dogs, comparatively innocent and gentle creatures? At any rate, " something must be done ; " the final argument always used, when a bad or desperate project is to be made palatable. So it was voted at last to send to Havana for an invoice of Spanish dogs, with their accompanying chasseurs; and the efforts at persuading the Maroons were postponed till the arrival of these additional persuasives. And when Col. Quarrell finally set sail as commissioner to obtain the new allies, all scruples of conscience

vanished in the renewal of public courage and
the chorus of popular gratitude ; a thing so
desirable must be right ; thrice they were
armed who knew their Quarrell just.

But after the parting notes of gratitude died
away in the distance, the commissioner began
to discover that he was to have a hard time
of it.   He sailed for Havana in a schooner
manned with Spanish renegadoes, who insisted
on fighting every thing that came in their
way, — first a Spanish schooner, then a French
one.   He landed at Batabano, struck across
the mountains towards Havana, stopped at
Besucal to call on the wealthy Marquesa de
San Felipe y San Jorge, grand patroness of
dogs and chasseurs, and finally was welcomed
to Havana by Don Luis de las Casas, who over-
looked, for this occasion only, an injunction
of his court against admitting foreigners within
his government; "the only accustomed exception being," as Don Luis courteously assured
him, " in favor of foreign traders who came
with new negroes."   To be sure, the commissioner had not brought any of these commodi-

ties; but then he had come to obtain the
means of capturing some, and so might pass
for an irregular practitioner of the privileged
profession.

Accordingly, Don Guillermo Dawes Quarrell
(so ran his passport) found no difficulty in
obtaining permission from the governor to buy
as many dogs as he desired. When, however,
he carelessly hinted at the necessity of taking,
also, a few men who should have care of the
dogs, — this being, after all, the essential part
of his expedition, — Don Luis de las Casas put
on instantly a double force of courtesy, and
assured him of the entire impossibility of
recruiting a single Spaniard for English
service. Finally, however, he gave permission
and passports for six chasseurs. Under cover
of this, the commissioner lost no time in
enlisting forty; he got them safe to Batabano;
but at the last moment, learning the state of
affairs, they refused to embark on such very
irregular authority. When he had persuaded
them, at length, the officer of the fort inter-
posed objections. This was not to be borne,

so Don Guillermo bribed him and silenced him; a dragoon was, however, sent to report to the governor; Don Guillermo sent a messenger after him, and bribed him too; and thus at length, after myriad rebuffs, and after being obliged to spend the last evening at a puppet-show in which the principal figure was a burlesque on his own personal peculiarities, the weary Don Guillermo, with his crew of renegadoes, and his forty chasseurs and their one hundred and four muzzled dogs, set sail for Jamaica.

These new allies were certainly something formidable, if we may trust the pictures and descriptions in Dallas's History. The chasseur was a tall, meagre, swarthy Spaniard or mulatto, lightly clad in cotton shirt and drawers, with broad straw hat, and moccasins of raw - hide; his belt sustaining his long, straight, flat sword or *machete*, like an iron bar sharpened at one end; and he wore by the same belt three cotton leashes for his three dogs, sometimes held also by chains. The dogs were a fierce breed, crossed between hound

and mastiff, never unmuzzled but for attack,
and accompanied by smaller dogs called *finders*.
It is no wonder, when these wild and powerful
creatures were landed at Montego Bay, that
terror ran through the town, doors were every-
where closed, and windows crowded; not a
negro dared to stir; and the muzzled dogs,
infuriated by confinement on shipboard, filled
the silent streets with their noisy barking and
the rattling of their chains.

How much would have come of all this in
actual conflict, does not appear. The Maroons
had already been persuaded to make peace
upon certain conditions and guaranties, — a
decision probably accelerated by the terrible
rumors of the bloodhounds, though they never
saw them. It was the declared opinion of
the Assembly, confirmed by that of Gen.
Walpole, that "nothing could be clearer than
that, if they had been off the island, the rebels
could not have been induced to surrender."
Nevertheless, a treaty was at last made, without
the direct intervention of the quadrupeds.
Again commissioners went up among the

mountains to treat with negotiators at first
invisible; again were hats and jackets interchanged, not without coy reluctance on the
part of the well-dressed Englishmen; and a
solemn agreement was effected. The most
essential part of the bargain was a guaranty
of continued independence, demanded by the
suspicious Maroons. Gen. Walpole, however,
promptly pledged himself that no such unfair
advantage should be taken of them as had
occurred with the hostages previously surrendered, who were placed in irons; nor should
any attempt be made to remove them from the
island. It is painful to add, that this promise
was outrageously violated by the Colonial Government, to the lasting grief of Gen. Walpole,
on the ground that the Maroons had violated
the treaty by a slight want of punctuality in
complying with its terms, and by remissness
in restoring the fugitive slaves who had taken
refuge among them. As many of the tribe
as surrendered, therefore, were at once placed
in confinement, and ultimately shipped from
Port Royal to Halifax, to the number of six

hundred, on the 6th of June, 1796. For the credit of English honor, we rejoice to know that Gen. Walpole not merely protested against this utter breach of faith, but indignantly declined the sword of honor which the Assembly had voted him, in its gratitude, and then retired from military service forever.

The remaining career of this portion of the Maroons is easily told. They were first dreaded by the inhabitants of Halifax, then welcomed when seen, and promptly set to work on the citadel, then in process of reconstruction, where the " Maroon Bastion " still remains, — their only visible memorial. Two commissioners had charge of them, one being the redoubtable Col. Quarrell ; and twenty-five thousand pounds were appropriated for their temporary support. Of course they did not prosper ; pensioned colonists never do, for they are not compelled into habits of industry. After their delicious life in the mountains of Jamaica, it seemed rather monotonous to dwell upon that barren soil, — for theirs was such that two previous colonies had deserted it, —

and in a climate where winter lasts seven
months in the year. They had a schoolmaster,
and he was also a preacher ; but they did not
seem to appreciate that luxury of civilization,
utterly refusing, on grounds of conscience, to
forsake polygamy, and, on grounds of personal
comfort, to listen to the doctrinal discourses of
their pastor, who was an ardent Sandemanian.
They smoked their pipes during service time,
and left Old Montagu, who still survived, to
lend a vicarious attention to the sermon. One
discourse he briefly reported as follows, very
much to the point : "Massa parson say no mus
tief, no mus meddle wid somebody wife, no
mus quarrel, mus set down softly." So they
sat down very softly, and showed an extreme
unwillingness to get up again. But, not being
naturally an idle race, — at least, in Jamaica the
objection lay rather on the other side, — they
soon grew tired of this inaction. Distrustful of
those about them, suspicious of all attempts
to scatter them among the community at large,
frozen by the climate, and constantly petition-
ing for removal to a milder one, they finally

wearied out all patience. A long dispute
ensued between the authorities of Nova Scotia
and Jamaica, as to which was properly respon-
sible for their support; and thus the heroic
race, that for a century and a half had sustained themselves in freedom in Jamaica, were
reduced to the position of troublesome and
impracticable paupers, shuttlecocks between
two selfish parishes. So passed their unfortunate lives, until, in 1800, their reduced population was transported to Sierra Leone, at a
cost of six thousand pounds; since which they
disappear from history.

It was judged best not to interfere with
those bodies of Maroons which had kept aloof
from the late outbreak, at the Accompong
settlement, and elsewhere.   They continued to
preserve a qualified independence, and retain
it even now. In 1835, two years after the
abolition of slavery in Jamaica, there were
reported sixty families of Maroons as residing
at Accompong Town, eighty families at Moore
Town, one hundred and ten families at Charles
Town, and twenty families at Scott Hall,

making two hundred and seventy families in all, — each station being, as of old, under the charge of a superintendent. But there can be little doubt, that, under the influences of freedom, they are rapidly intermingling with the mass of colored population in Jamaica.

The story of the exiled Maroons attracted attention in high quarters, in its time: the wrongs done to them were denounced in Parliament by Sheridan, and mourned by Wilberforce; while the employment of bloodhounds against them was vindicated by Dundas, and the whole conduct of the Colonial Government defended, through thick and thin, by Bryan Edwards. This thorough partisan even had the assurance to tell Mr. Wilberforce, in Parliament, that he knew the Maroons, from personal knowledge, to be cannibals, and that, if a missionary were sent among them in Nova Scotia, they would immediately eat him; a charge so absurd that he did not venture to repeat it in his History of the West Indies, though his injustice to the Maroons is even there so glaring as to provoke the indignation

of the more moderate Dallas. But, in spite
of Mr. Edwards, the public indignation ran
quite high in England, against the bloodhounds
and their employers, so that the home ministry
found it necessary to send a severe reproof to
the Colonial Government. For a few years the
tales of the Maroons thus emerged from mere
colonial annals, and found their way into
annual registers and parliamentary debates;
but they have long since vanished from popular
memory. Their record still retains its interest,
however, as that of one of the heroic races
of the world; and all the more, because it is
with their kindred that the American nation
has to deal, in solving one of the most
momentous problems of its future career.

THE MAROONS OF SURINAM.

WHEN that eccentric individual, Capt. John Gabriel Stedman, resigned his commission in the English Navy, took the oath of abjuration, and was appointed ensign in the Scots brigade employed for two centuries by Holland, he little knew that "their High Mightinesses the States of the United Provinces" would send him out, within a year, to the forests of Guiana, to subdue rebel negroes. He never imagined that the year 1773 would behold him beneath the rainy season in a tropical country, wading through marshes and splashing through lakes, exploring with his feet for submerged paths, commanding impracticable troops, and commanded by an insufferable colonel, feeding on greegree worms and fed upon by mosquitos, howled at by jaguars, hissed at by serpents, and shot at by those exceedingly

unattainable gentlemen, "still longed for, never
seen," the Maroons of Surinam.

Yet, as our young ensign sailed up the Surinam River, the world of tropic beauty came
upon him with enchantment.   Dark, moist verdure was close around him, rippling waters
below; the tall trees of the jungle and the low
mangroves beneath were all hung with long
vines and lianas, a maze of cordage, like a fleet
at anchor; lithe monkeys travelled ceaselessly
up and down these airy paths, in armies, bearing their young, like knapsacks, on their backs;
macaws and humming-birds, winged jewels, flew
from tree to tree.   As they neared Paramaribo,
the river became a smooth canal among luxu-
riant plantations; the air was perfumed music,
redolent of orange-blossoms and echoing with
the songs of birds and the sweet plash of oars;
gay barges came forth to meet them; "while
groups of naked boys and girls were promis-
cuously playing and flouncing, like so many
tritons and mermaids, in the water."   And
when the troops disembarked, — five hundred
fine young men, the oldest not thirty, all arrayed

in new uniforms and bearing orange-flowers in
their caps, a bridal wreath for beautiful Guiana,
— it is no wonder that the Creole ladies were
in ecstasy; and the boyish recruits little fore-
saw the day, when, reduced to a few dozens,
barefooted and ragged as filibusters, their last
survivors would gladly re-embark from a country beside which even Holland looked dry and
even Scotland comfortable.

For over all that earthly paradise there
brooded not alone its terrible malaria, its days
of fever and its nights of deadly chill, but the
worse shadows of oppression and of sin, which
neither day nor night could banish. The first
object which met Stedman's eye, as he stepped
on shore, was the figure of a young girl stripped
to receive two hundred lashes, and chained to
a hundred-pound weight. And the few first
days gave a glimpse into a state of society
worthy of this exhibition, — men without mercy,
women without modesty, the black man a slave
to the white man's passions, and the white man
a slave to his own. The later West-Indian
society in its worst forms is probably a mere

dilution of the utter profligacy of those early days. Greek or Roman decline produced nothing more debilitating or destructive than the ordinary life of a Surinam planter, and his one virtue of hospitality only led to more unbridled excesses and completed the work of vice. No wonder that Stedman himself, who, with all his peculiarities, was essentially simple and manly, soon became disgusted, and made haste to get into the woods and cultivate the society of the Maroons.

The rebels against whom this expedition was sent were not the original Maroons of Surinam, but a later generation. The originals had long since established their independence, and their leaders were flourishing their honorary silver-mounted canes in the streets of Paramaribo. Fugitive negroes had begun to establish themselves in the woods from the time when the colony was finally ceded by the English to the Dutch, in 1674. The first open outbreak occurred in 1726, when the plantations on the Seramica River revolted; it was found impossible to subdue them, and the government very

imprudently resolved to make an example of
eleven captives, and thus terrify the rest of the
rebels. They were tortured to death, eight of
the eleven being women : this drove the others
to madness, and plantation after plantation was
visited with fire and sword. After a long conflict, their chief, Adoe, was induced to make a
treaty, in 1749. The rebels promised to keep
the peace, and in turn were promised freedom,
money, tools, clothes, and, finally, arms and
ammunition.

But no permanent peace was ever made upon
a barrel of gunpowder as a basis; and, of
course, an explosion followed this one. The
colonists naturally evaded the last item of the
bargain ; and the rebels, receiving the gifts, and
remarking the omission of the part of Hamlet,
asked contemptuously if the Europeans expected negroes to subsist on combs and look-
ing-glasses ? New hostilities at once began ;
a new body of slaves on the Ouca River revolted ; the colonial government was changed
in consequence, and fresh troops shipped from
Holland ; and after four different embassies

had been sent into the woods, the rebels began to listen to reason. The black generals, Capt. Araby and Capt. Boston, agreed upon a truce for a year, during which the colonial government might decide for peace or war, the Maroons declaring themselves indifferent. Finally the government chose peace, delivered ammunition, and made a treaty, in 1761; the white and black plenipotentiaries exchanged English oaths and then negro oaths, each tasting a drop of the other's blood during the latter ceremony, amid a volley of remarkable incantations from the black *gadoman* or priest. After some final skirmishes, in which the rebels almost always triumphed, the treaty was at length accepted by all the various villages of Maroons. Had they known that at this very time five thousand slaves in Berbice were just rising against their masters, and were looking to them for assistance, the result might have been different; but this fact had not reached them, nor had the rumors of insurrection in Brazil among negro and Indian slaves. They consented, therefore, to the peace. " They

write from Surinam," says the "Annual Register" for Jan. 23, 1761, "that the Dutch governor, finding himself unable to subdue the
rebel negroes of that country by force, hath
wisely followed the example of Gov. Trelawney
at Jamaica, and concluded an amicable treaty
with them; in consequence of which, all the
negroes of the woods are acknowledged to be
free, and all that is passed is buried in oblivion." So ended a war of thirty-six years; and
in Stedman's day the original three thousand
Ouca and Seramica Maroons had multiplied,
almost incredibly, to fifteen thousand.

But for those slaves not sharing in this revolt
it was not so easy to "bury the whole past in
oblivion." The Maroons had told some very
plain truths to the white ambassadors, and had
frankly advised them, if they wished for peace,
to mend their own manners and treat their
chattels humanely. But the planters learned
nothing by experience, — and, indeed, the terrible narrations of Stedman were confirmed by
those of Alexander, so lately as 1831. Of
course, therefore, in a colony comprising eighty

thousand blacks to four thousand whites, other
revolts were stimulated by the success of this
one. They reached their highest point in 1772,
when an insurrection on the Cottica River, led
by a negro named Baron, almost gave the finish-
ing blow to the colony ; the only adequate protection being found in a body of slaves liberated
expressly for that purpose, — a dangerous and
humiliating precedent. " We have been obliged
to set three or four hundred of our stoutest
negroes free to defend us," says an honest letter
from Surinam, in the " Annual Register " for
Sept. 5, 1772. Fortunately for the safety of
the planters, Baron presumed too much upon
his numbers, and injudiciously built a camp
too near the seacoast, in a marshy fastness,
from which he was finally ejected by twelve
hundred Dutch troops, though the chief work
was done, Stedman thinks, by the " black
rangers " or liberated slaves. Checked by this
defeat, he again drew back into the forests,
resuming his guerrilla warfare against the plantations. Nothing could dislodge him ; bloodhounds were proposed, but the moisture of the

country made them useless: and thus matters
stood when Stedman came sailing, amid orange-
blossoms and music, up the winding Surinam.

Our young officer went into the woods in the
condition of Falstaff, " heinously unprovided."
Coming from the unbounded luxury of the
plantations, he found himself entering "the
most horrid and impenetrable forests, where no
kind of refreshment was to be had," — he being
provisioned only with salt pork and pease.
After a wail of sorrow for this inhuman
neglect, he bursts into a gush of gratitude for
the private generosity which relieved his wants
at the last moment by the following list of
supplies: " 24 bottles best claret, 12 ditto
Madeira, 12 ditto porter, 12 ditto cider, 12
ditto rum, 2 large loaves white sugar, 2 gallons
brandy, 6 bottles muscadel, 2 gallons lemon-
juice, 2 gallons ground coffee, 2 large West-
phalia hams, 2 salted bullocks' tongues, 1 bottle
Durham mustard, 6 dozen spermaceti candles."
The hams and tongues seem, indeed, rather a
poor halfpennyworth to this intolerable deal of
sack ; but this instance of Surinam privation in

those days may open some glimpse at the colonial standards of comfort. " From this specimen," moralizes our hero, " the reader will easily perceive, that, if some of the inhabitants of Surinam show themselves the disgrace of the creation by their cruelties and brutality, others, by their social feelings, approve themselves an ornament to the human species. With this instance of virtue and generosity I therefore conclude this chapter."

But the troops soon had to undergo worse troubles than those of the commissariat. The rainy season had just set in. " As for the negroes," said Mr. Klynhaus, the last planter with whom they parted, " you may depend on never seeing a soul of them, unless they attack you off guard ; but the climate, the climate, will murder you all." Bringing with them constitutions already impaired by the fevers and dissipation of Paramaribo, the poor boys began to perish long before they began to fight. Wading in water all day, hanging their hammocks over water at night, it seemed a moist existence, even compared with the climate of Eng-

land and the soil of Holland. It was a case of
" Invent a shovel, and be a magistrate," even
more than Andrew Marvell found it in the
United Provinces. In fact, Raynal evidently
thinks that nothing but Dutch experience in
hydraulics could ever have cultivated Surinam.

The two gunboats which held one division
of the expedition were merely old sugar-barges,
roofed over with boards, and looking like coffins. They were pleasantly named the "Charon" and the "Cerberus," but Stedman
thought that the "Sudden Death" and the
" Wilful Murder" would have been titles
more appropriate. The chief duty of the
troops consisted in lying at anchor at the
intersections of wooded streams, waiting for
rebels who never came. It was dismal work,
and the raw recruits were full of the same
imaginary terrors which have haunted other
heroes less severely tested: the monkeys never
rattled the cocoa-nuts against the trees, but
they all heard the axes of Maroon wood-
choppers; and when a sentinel declared, one
night, that he had seen a negro go down the

river in a canoe, with his pipe lighted, the
whole force was called to arms — against a
firefly. In fact, the insect race brought by
far the most substantial dangers. The rebels
eluded the military, but the chigres, locusts,
scorpions, and bush-spiders were ever ready
to come half-way to meet them ; likewise serpents and alligators proffered them the freedom of the forests, and exhibited a hospitality almost excessive. Snakes twenty feet long
hung their seductive length from the trees ;
jaguars volunteered their society through
almost impenetrable marshes ; vampire bats
perched by night with lulling endearments
upon the toes of the soldiers. When Stedman describes himself as killing thirty-eight
mosquitoes at one stroke, we must perhaps
pardon something to the spirit of martyrdom.
But when we add to these the other woes of
his catalogue, — prickly-heat, ringworm, putrid-
fever, "the growling of Col. Fougeaud, dry
sandy savannas, unfordable marshes, burning
hot days, cold and damp nights, heavy rains,
and short allowance," — we can hardly wonder

that three captains died in a month, and that in two months his detachment of forty-two was reduced to a miserable seven.

Yet, through all this, Stedman himself kept his health. His theory of the matter almost recalls the time-honored prescription of "A light heart and a thin pair of breeches," for he attributes his good condition to his keeping up his spirits and kicking off his shoes. Daily bathing in the river had also something to do with it; and, indeed, hydropathy was first learned of the West-India Maroons, — who did their "packing" in wet clay, — and was carried by Dr. Wright to England. But his extraordinary personal qualities must have contributed most to his preservation. Never did a "meagre, starved, black, burnt, and ragged tatterdemalion," as he calls himself, carry about him such a fund of sentiment, philosophy, poetry, and art. He had a great faculty for sketching, as the engravings in his volumes, with all their odd peculiarities, show; his deepest woes he coined always into couplets, and fortified himself against hopeless

despair with Ovid and Valerius Flaccus, Pope's
Homer and Thomson's " Seasons." Above all
reigned his passion for natural history, a ready
balm for every ill. Here he was never want-
ing to the occasion; and, to do justice to
Dutch Guiana, the occasion never was want-
ing to him. Were his men sickening, the
peccaries were always healthy without the
camp, and the cockroaches within; just escap-
ing from a she-jaguar, he satisfies himself, ere
he flees, that the print of her claws on the
sand is precisely the size of a pewter dinner-
plate ; bitten by a scorpion, he makes sure of
a scientific description in case he should expire of the bite; is the water undrinkable,
there is at least some rational interest in the
number of legs possessed by the centipedes
which pre-occupy it. This is the highest triumph of man over his accidents, when he thus
turns his pains to gains, and becomes an ento-
mologist in the tropics.

Meanwhile the rebels kept their own course
in the forests, and occasionally descended upon
plantations beside the very river on whose

upper waters the useless troops were sickening and dying. Stedman himself made several
campaigns, with long intervals of illness, before
he came any nearer to the enemy than to burn
a deserted village or destroy a rice-field. Sometimes they left the " Charon " and the "Cerberus" moored by grape-vines to the pine-trees,
and made expeditions into the woods, single file.
Our ensign, true to himself, gives the minutest
schedule of the order of march, and the oddest
little diagram of manikins with cocked hats,
and blacker manikins bearing burdens. First,
negroes with bill-hooks to clear the way ; then
the van-guard ; then the main body, inter-
spersed with negroes bearing boxes of ball-
cartridges ; then the rear-guard, with many
more negroes, bearing camp-equipage, provisions, and new rum, surnamed " kill-devil," and
appropriately followed by a sort of palanquin
for the disabled. Thus arrayed, they marched
valorously forth into the woods, to some given
point ; then they turned, marched back to the
boats, then rowed back to camp, and straight-
way went into the hospital. Immediately upon

this, the coast being clear, Baron and his rebels marched out again, and proceeded to business.

In the course of years, these Maroons had acquired their own peculiar tactics. They built stockaded fortresses on marshy islands, accessible by fords which they alone could traverse. These they defended further by sharp wooden pins, or crows'-feet, concealed beneath the surface of the miry ground, — and, latterly, by the more substantial protection of cannon, which they dragged into the woods, and learned to use. Their bush-fighting was unique. Having always more men than weapons, they arranged their warriors in threes, — one to use the musket, another to take his place if wounded or slain, and a third to drag away the body. They had Indian stealthiness and swiftness, with more than Indian discipline; discharged their fire with some approach to regularity, in three successive lines, the signals being given by the captain's horn. They were full of ingenuity: marked their movements for each other by scattered leaves and blazed trees; ran zigzag, to dodge bullets ; gave wooden guns

to their unarmed men, to frighten the plantation negroes on their guerrilla expeditions; and
borrowed the red caps of the black rangers
whom they slew, to bewilder the aim of the
others. One of them, finding himself close to
the muzzle of a ranger's gun, threw up his hand
hastily. "What!" he exclaimed, "will you
fire on one of your own party?" "God
forbid!" cried the ranger, dropping his piece,
and was instantly shot through the body by the
Maroon, who the next instant had disappeared
in the woods.

These rebels were no saints: their worship
was obi-worship; the women had not far out-
grown the plantation standard of chastity, and
the men drank "kill-devil" like their betters.
Stedman was struck with the difference between
the meaning of the word "good" in rebellious
circles and in reputable. "It must, however,
be observed, that what we Europeans call a good
character was by the Africans looked upon as
detestable, especially by those born in the
woods, whose only crime consisted in avenging
the wrongs done to their forefathers." But if

martial virtues be virtues, such were theirs.
Not a rebel ever turned traitor or informer, ever
flinched in battle or under torture, ever violated
a treaty or even a private promise. But it was
their power of endurance which was especially
astounding; Stedman is never weary of paying
tribute to this, or of illustrating it in sickening
detail; indeed, the records of the world show
nothing to surpass it; "the lifted axe, the
agonizing wheel," proved powerless to subdue
it; with every limb lopped, every bone broken,
the victims yet defied their tormentors, laughed,
sang, and died triumphant.

Of course they repaid these atrocities in
kind. If they had not, it would have demonstrated the absurd paradox, that slavery edu-
cates higher virtues than freedom. It bewilders
all the relations of human responsibility, if we
expect the insurrectionary slave to commit no
outrages; if slavery has not depraved him, it
has done him little harm. If it be the normal
tendency of bondage to produce saints like
Uncle Tom, let us all offer ourselves at auction
immediately. It is Cassy and Dred who are

the normal protest of human nature against systems which degrade it. Accordingly, these poor, ignorant Maroons, who had seen their brothers and sisters flogged, burned, mutilated, hanged on iron hooks, broken on the wheel, and had been all the while solemnly assured that this was paternal government, could only repay the paternalism in the same fashion, when they had the power. Stedman saw a negro chained to a red-hot distillery-furnace; he saw disobedient slaves, in repeated instances, punished by the amputation of a leg, and sent to boat-service for the rest of their lives; and of course the rebels borrowed these suggestions. They could bear to watch their captives expire under the lash, for they had previously watched their parents. If the government rangers received twenty-five florins for every rebel right-hand which they brought in, of course they risked their own right hands in the pursuit. The difference was, that the one brutality was that of a mighty state, and the other was only the retaliation of the victims. And after all, Stedman never ven-

tures to assert that the imitation equalled the
original, or that the Maroons had inflicted
nearly so much as they had suffered.

The leaders of the rebels, especially, were
men who had each his own story of wrongs
to tell. Baron, the most formidable, had been
the slave of a Swedish gentleman, who had
taught him to read and write, taken him to
Europe, promised to manumit him on his
return — and then, breaking his word, sold
him to a Jew. Baron refused to work for his
new master, was publicly flogged under the
gallows, fled to the woods next day, and became
the terror of the colony. Joli Cœur, his first
captain, was avenging the cruel wrongs of his
mother. Bonny, another leader, was born in
the woods, his mother having taken refuge
there just previously, to escape from his father,
who was also his master. Cojo, another, had
defended his master against the insurgents
until he was obliged by ill usage to take
refuge among them; and he still bore upon
his wrist, when Stedman saw him, a silver
band, with the inscription, — " True to the

Europeans." In dealing with wrongs like these, Mr. Carlyle would have found the despised negroes quite as ready as himself to take the total-abstinence pledge against rose-water.

In his first two-months' campaign, Stedman never saw the trace of a Maroon; in the second, he once came upon their trail; in the third, one captive was brought in, two surrendered themselves voluntarily, and a large party was found to have crossed a river within a mile of the camp, ferrying themselves on palm-trunks, according to their fashion. Deep swamps and scorching sands, toiling through briers all day, and sleeping at night in hammocks suspended over stagnant water, with weapons supported on sticks crossed beneath, — all this was endured for two years and a half, before Stedman personally came in sight of the enemy.

On Aug. 20, 1775, the troops found themselves at last in the midst of the rebel settlements. These villages and forts bore a variety of expressive names, such as " Hide me. O

thou surrounding verdure," "I shall be taken,"
"The woods lament for me," "Disturb me, if
you dare," "Take a tasting, if you like it,"
"Come, try me, if you be men," "God knows
me, and none else," "I shall moulder before I
shall be taken." Some were only plantation-
grounds with a few huts, and were easily laid
waste; but all were protected more or less by
their mere situations. Quagmires surrounded
them, covered by a thin crust of verdure, sometimes broken through by one man's weight,
when the victim sank hopelessly into the black
and bottomless depths below. In other directions there was a solid bottom, but inconven-
iently covered by three or four feet of water,
through which the troops waded breast-deep,
holding their muskets high in the air, unable
to reload them when once discharged, and
liable to be picked off by rebel scouts, who
ingeniously posted themselves in the tops of
palm-trees.

Through this delectable region Col. Fougeaud
and his followers slowly advanced, drawing
near the fatal shore where Capt. Meyland's

detachment had just been defeated, and where their mangled remains still polluted the beach. Passing this point of danger without attack, they suddenly met a small party of rebels, each bearing on his back a beautifully woven hamper of snow-white rice: these loads they threw down, and disappeared. Next appeared an armed body from the same direction, who fired upon them once, and swiftly retreated; and in a few moments the soldiers came upon a large field of standing rice, beyond which lay, like an amphitheatre, the rebel village. But between the village and the field had been piled successive defences of logs and branches, behind which simple redoubts the Maroons lay concealed. A fight ensued, lasting forty minutes, during which nearly every soldier and ranger was wounded; but, to their great amazement, not one was killed. This was an enigma to them until after the skirmish, when the surgeon found that most of them had been struck, not by bullets, but by various substitutes, such as pebbles, coat-buttons, and bits of silver coin, which had penetrated only skin deep. "We

also observed that several of the poor rebel
negroes, who had been shot, had only the shards
of Spa-water cans instead of flints, which could
seldom do execution; and it was certainly
owing to these circumstances that we came off
so well."

The rebels at length retreated, first setting
fire to their village; a hundred or more lightly
built houses, some of them two stories high,
were soon in flames; and as this conflagration
occupied the only neck of land between two
impassable morasses, the troops were unable to
follow, and the Maroons had left nothing but
rice-fields to be pillaged. That night the military force was encamped in the woods; their
ammunition was almost gone, so they were
ordered to lie flat on the ground, even in case
of attack; they could not so much as build a
fire. Before midnight an attack was made on
them, partly with bullets, and partly with
words. The Maroons were all around them in
the forest, but their object was a puzzle; they
spent most of the night in bandying compliments with the black rangers, whom they alter-

nately denounced, ridiculed, and challenged to single combat. At last Fougeaud and Stedman joined in the conversation, and endeavored to make this midnight volley of talk the occasion for a treaty. This was received with inextinguishable laughter, which echoed through the woods like a concert of screech-owls, ending in a *charivari* of horns and hallooing. The colonel, persisting, offered them "life, liberty, victuals, drink, and all they wanted;" in return, they ridiculed him unmercifully. He was a half-starved Frenchman, who had run away from his own country, and would soon run away from theirs; they profoundly pitied him and his soldiers; they would scorn to spend powder on such scarecrows; they would rather feed and clothe them, as being poor white slaves, hired to be shot at, and starved for fourpence a day. But as for the planters, overseers, and rangers, they should die, every one of them, and Bonny should be governor of the colony. "After this, they tinkled their bill-hooks, fired a volley, and gave three cheers; which, being answered by the rangers, the clamor ended, and the rebels dispersed with the rising sun."

Very aimless nonsense it certainly appeared. But the next day put a new aspect on it ; for it was found, that, under cover of all this noise, the Maroons had been busily occupied all night, men, women, and children, in preparing and filling great hampers of the finest rice, yams, and cassava, from the adjacent provision-grounds, to be used for subsistence during their escape, leaving only chaff and refuse for the hungry soldiers. "This was certainly such a masterly trait of generalship in a savage people, whom we affected to despise, as would have done honor to any European commander."

From this time the Maroons fulfilled their threats. Shooting down without mercy every black ranger who came within their reach, — one of these rangers being, in Stedman's estimate, worth six white soldiers, — they left Col. Fougeaud and his regulars to die of starvation and fatigue. The enraged colonel, "finding himself thus foiled by a naked negro, swore he

would pursue Bonny to the world's end." But
he never got any nearer than to Bonny's
kitchen-gardens. He put the troops on half-
allowance, sent back for provisions and ammunition, — and within ten days changed his
mind, and retreated to the settlements in
despair. Soon after, this very body of rebels,
under Bonny's leadership, plundered two plantations in the vicinity, and nearly captured a
powder-magazine, which was, however, suc-
cessfully defended by some armed slaves.

For a year longer these expeditions continued. The troops never gained a victory,
and they lost twenty men for every rebel
killed ; but they gradually checked the plunder
of plantations, destroyed villages and planting-
grounds, and drove the rebels, for the time
at least, into the deeper recesses of the woods,
or into the adjacent province of Cayenne.
They had the slight satisfaction of burning
Bonny's own house, a two-story wooden hut,
built in the fashion of our frontier guard-
houses. They often took single prisoners, —
some child, born and bred in the woods, and

frightened equally by the first sight of a white
man and of a cow, — or some warrior, who, on
being threatened with torture, stretched forth
both hands in disdain, and said, with Indian
eloquence, "These hands have made tigers
tremble." As for Stedman, he still went barefooted, still quarrelled with his colonel, still
sketched the scenery and described the reptiles,
still reared greegree worms for his private
kitchen, still quoted good poetry and wrote
execrable, still pitied all the sufferers around
him, black, white, and red, until finally he and
his comrades were ordered back to Holland in
1776.

Among all that wasted regiment of weary
and broken-down men, there was probably no
one but Stedman who looked backward with
longing as they sailed down the lovely Surinam.
True, he bore all his precious collections with
him, — parrots and butterflies, drawings on the
backs of old letters, and journals kept on bones
and cartridges. But he had left behind him a
dearer treasure ; for there runs through all his
eccentric narrative a single thread of pure

romance, in his love for his beautiful quadroon wife and his only son.

Within a month after his arrival in the colony, our susceptible ensign first saw Joanna, a slave-girl of fifteen, at the house of an intimate friend. Her extreme beauty and modesty first fascinated him, and then her piteous narrative, — for she was the daughter of a planter, who had just gone mad and died in despair from the discovery that he could not legally emancipate his own children from slavery. Soon after, Stedman was dangerously ill, was neglected and alone; fruits and cordials were anonymously sent to him, which proved at last to have come from Joanna; and she came herself, ere long, and nursed him, grateful for the visible sympathy he had shown to her. This completed the conquest; the passionate young Englishman, once recovered, loaded her with presents which she refused; talked of purchasing her, and educating her in Europe, which she also declined as burdening him too greatly; and finally, amid the ridicule of all good society in Paramaribo, surmounted all legal obstacles, and was united to the beautiful girl in honorable marriage. He provided a cottage for her, where he spent his furloughs, in perfect happiness, for four years.

The simple idyl of their loves was unbroken by any stain or disappointment, and yet always shadowed with the deepest anxiety for the future. Though treated with the utmost indulgence, she was legally a slave, and so was the boy of whom she became the mother. Cojo, her uncle, was a captain among the rebels against whom her husband fought. And up to the time when Stedman was ordered back to Holland, he was unable to purchase her freedom; nor could he, until the very last moment, procure the emancipation of his boy. His perfect delight at this last triumph, when obtained, elicited some satire from his white friends. " While the well-thinking few highly applauded my sensibility, many not only blamed but publicly derided me for my paternal affection, which was called a weakness, a whim." " Nearly forty beautiful boys and girls were left to perpetual slavery by their parents

of my acquaintance, and many of them without
being so much as once inquired after at all."

But Stedman was a true-hearted fellow, if his
sentiment did sometimes run to rodomontade;
he left his Joanna only in the hope that a year
or two in Europe would repair his ruined for-
tunes, and he could return to treat himself to
the purchase of his own wedded wife. He
describes, with unaffected pathos, their parting
scene, — though, indeed, there were several successive partings, — and closes the description
in a characteristic manner: " My melancholy
having surpassed all description, I at last determined to weather one or two painful years
in her absence; and in the afternoon went to
dissipate my mind at a Mr. Roux' cabinet of
Indian curiosities; where, as my eye chanced
to fall on a rattlesnake, I will, before I leave
the colony, describe this dangerous reptile."

It was impossible to write the history of the
Maroons of Surinam except through the biog-
raphy of our ensign (at last promoted captain),
because nearly all we know of them is through
his quaint and picturesque narrative, with its

profuse illustrations by his own hand. It is
not fair, therefore, to end without chronicling
his safe arrival in Holland, on June 3, 1777.
It is a remarkable fact, that, after his life in
the woods, even the Dutch looked slovenly
to his eyes. "The inhabitants, who crowded
about us, appeared but a disgusting assemblage
of ill-formed and ill-dressed rabble, — so much
had my prejudices been changed by living
among Indians and blacks: their eyes seemed
to resemble those of a pig; their complexions
were like the color of foul linen; they seemed
to have no teeth, and to be covered over with
rags and dirt. This prejudice, however, was
not against these people only, but against all
Europeans in general, when compared to the
sparkling eyes, ivory teeth, shining skin, and
remarkable cleanliness of those I had left
behind me." Yet, in spite of these superior
attractions, he never recrossed the Atlantic;
for his Joanna died soon after, and his promis-
ing son, being sent to the father, was educated
in England, became a midshipman in the navy,
and was lost at sea. With his elegy, in which

the last depths of bathos are sadly sounded by
a mourning parent, — who is induced to print
them only by "the effect they had on the
sympathetic and ingenious Mrs. Cowley," —
the "Narrative of a Five Years' Expedition"
closes.

The war, which had cost the government
forty thousand pounds a year, was ended, and
left both parties essentially as when it began.
The Maroons gradually returned to their old
abodes, and, being unmolested themselves, left
others unmolested thenceforward. Originally
three thousand, — in Stedman's time, fifteen
thousand, — they were estimated at seventy
thousand by Capt. Alexander, who saw Guiana
in 1831; and a later American scientific expedition, having visited them in their homes,
reported them as still enjoying their wild freedom, and multiplying, while the Indians on the
same soil decay. The beautiful forests of Surinam still make the morning gorgeous with their
beauty, and the night deadly with their chill;
the stately palm still rears, a hundred feet in
air, its straight gray shaft and its head of

verdure; the mora builds its solid, buttressed
trunk, a pedestal for the eagle; the pine of the
tropics holds out its myriad hands with water-
cups for the rain and dews, where all the birds
and the monkeys may drink their fill; the
trees are garlanded with epiphytes and con-
volvuli, and anchored to the earth by a thousand vines. High among their branches, the
red and yellow mocking-birds still build their
hanging nests, uncouth storks and tree-porcu-
pines cling above, and the spotted deer and
the tapir drink from the sluggish stream below.
The night is still made noisy with a thousand
cries of bird and beast; and the stillness of the
sultry noon is broken by the slow tolling of
the *campañero*, or bell-bird, far in the deep,
dark woods, like the chime of some lost con-
vent. And as Nature is unchanged there, so
apparently is man; the Maroons still retain
their savage freedom, still shoot their wild
game and trap their fish, still raise their rice
and cassava, yams and plantains, — still make
cups from the gourd-tree and hammocks from
the silk-grass plant, wine from the palm-tree's

sap, brooms from its leaves, fishing-lines from its fibres, and salt from its ashes. Their life does not yield, indeed, the very highest results of spiritual culture; its mental and moral results may not come up to the level of civilization, but they rise far above the level of slavery. In the changes of time, the Maroons may yet elevate themselves into the one, but they will never relapse into the other.

GABRIEL'S DEFEAT

IN exploring among dusty files of newspapers
for the true records of Denmark Vesey
and Nat Turner, I have caught occasional
glimpses of a plot perhaps more wide in its
outlines than that of either, which has lain
obscure in the darkness of half a century,
traceable only in the political events which
dated from it, and the utter incorrectness of
the scanty traditions which assumed to preserve it. And though researches in public
libraries have only proved to me how rapidly
the materials for American history are vanish-
ing, — since not one of our great institutions
possessed, a few years since, a file of any
Southern newspaper of the year 1800, — yet
the little which I have gained may have an
interest that makes it worth preserving.

Three times, at intervals of thirty years,

did a wave of unutterable terror sweep across
the Old Dominion, bringing thoughts of agony
to every Virginian master, and of vague hope
to every Virginian slave. Each time did one
man's name become a spell of dismay and a
symbol of deliverance. Each time did that
name eclipse its predecessor, while recalling
it for a moment to fresher memory: John
Brown revived the story of Nat Turner, as
in his day Nat Turner recalled the vaster
schemes of Gabriel.

On Sept. 8, 1800, a Virginia correspondent
wrote thus to the Philadelphia *United - States
Gazette : —*

"For the week past, we have been under
momentary expectation of a rising among the
negroes, who have assembled to the number of
nine hundred or a thousand, and threatened to
massacre all the whites. They are armed with
desperate weapons, and secrete themselves in
the woods. God only knows our fate: we
have strong guards every night under arms."

It was no wonder, if there were foundation
for such rumors. Liberty was the creed or the

cant of the day. France was being disturbed
by revolution, and England by Clarkson. In
America, slavery was habitually recognized as
a misfortune and an error, only to be palliated
by the nearness of its expected end. How
freely anti-slavery pamphlets had been circulated in Virginia, we know from the priceless
volumes collected and annotated by Washington, and now preserved in the Boston
Athenæum. Jefferson's " Notes on Virginia,"
itself an anti-slavery tract, had passed through
seven editions. Judge St. George Tucker,
law-professor in William and Mary College,
had recently published his noble work, " A
Dissertation on Slavery, with a Proposal for
the Gradual Abolition of it in the State of
Virginia." From all this agitation, a slave
insurrection was a mere corollary. With so
much electricity in the air, a single flash of
lightning foreboded all the terrors of the tempest. Let but a single armed negro be seen or
suspected, and at once, on many a lonely plantation, there were trembling hands at work to
bar doors and windows that seldom had been

even closed before, and there was shuddering
when a gray squirrel scrambled over the roof,
or a shower of walnuts came down clattering
from the overhanging boughs.

Early in September, 1800, as a certain Mr.
Moseley Sheppard, of Henrico County in Virginia, was one day sitting in his counting-room,
two negroes knocked at the door, and were let
in. They shut the door themselves, and began
to unfold an insurrectionary plot, which was
subsequently repeated by one of them, named
Ben Woodfolk or Woolfolk, in presence of the
court, on the 15th of the same month.

He stated, that about the first of the preced-
ing June, he had been asked by a negro named
Colonel George whether he would like to be
made a Mason. He refused; but George ultimately prevailed on him to have an interview
with a certain leading man among the blacks,
named Gabriel. Arrived at the place of meeting, he found many persons assembled, to whom
a preliminary oath was administered, that they
would keep secret all which they might hear.
The leaders then began, to the dismay of this

witness, to allude to a plan of insurrection,
which, as they stated, was already far advanced
toward maturity.   Presently a man named
Martin, Gabriel's brother, proposed religious
services, caused the company to be duly seated,
and began an impassioned exposition of Scripture, bearing upon the perilous theme.   The
Israelites were glowingly portrayed as a type
of successful resistance to tyranny; and it was
argued, that now, as then, God would stretch
forth his arm to save, and would strengthen a
hundred to overthrow a thousand.   Thus passed,
the witness stated, this preparatory meeting.
At a subsequent gathering the affair was
brought to a point; and the only difficult question was, whether to rise in rebellion upon a
certain Saturday, or upon the Sunday following.
Gabriel said that Saturday was the day already
fixed, and that it must not be altered; but
George was for changing it to Sunday, as being
more convenient for the country negroes, who
could travel on that day without suspicion.
Gabriel, however, said decisively that they had
enough to carry Richmond without them; and

Saturday was therefore retained as the momentous day.

This was the confession, so far as it is now
accessible; and on the strength of it, Ben
Woolfolk was promptly pardoned by the court
for all his sins, past, present, or to come,
and they proceeded with their investigation.
Of Gabriel little appeared to be known, except that he had been the property of Thomas
Prosser, a young man who had recently in-
herited a plantation a few miles from Richmond, and who had the reputation among his
neighbors of " behaving with great barbarity to
his slaves." Gabriel was, however, reported
to be "a fellow of courage and intellect above
his rank in life," to be about twenty-five years
of age, and to be guiltless of the alphabet.

Further inquiry made it appear that the
preparations of the insurgents were hardly adequate to any grand revolutionary design, — at
least, if they proposed to begin with open warfare. The commissariat may have been well
organized, for black Virginians are apt to have
a prudent eye to the larder; but the ordnance

department and the treasury were as low as if Secretary Floyd had been in charge of them. A slave called "Prosser's Ben" testified that he went with Gabriel to see Ben Woolfolk, who was going to Caroline County to enlist men, and that "Gabriel gave him three shillings for himself and three other negroes, to be expended in recruiting men." Their arms and ammunition, so far as reported, consisted of a peck of bullets, ten pounds of powder, and twelve scythe-swords, made by Gabriel's brother Solomon, and fitted with handles by Gabriel himself. "These cutlasses," said subsequently a white eye-witness, "are made of scythes cut in two and fixed into well-turned handles. I have never seen arms so murderous. Those who still doubt the importance of the conspiracy which has been so fortunately frustrated would shudder with horror at the sight of these instruments of death." And as it presently appeared that a conspirator named Scott had astonished his master by accidentally pulling ten dollars from a ragged pocket which seemed inade-

quate to the custody of ten cents, it was
agreed that the plot might still be dangerous, even though the resources seemed limited.

And indeed, as was soon discovered, the effec-
tive weapon of the insurgents lay in the very
audacity of their plan. If the current statements of all the Virginia letter-writers were
true, " nothing could have been better con-
trived." It was to have taken effect on the first
day of September. The rendezvous for the
blacks was to be a brook six miles from Richmond. Eleven hundred men were to assemble
there, and were to be divided into three columns,
their officers having been designated in advance.
All were to march on Richmond, — then a town
of eight thousand inhabitants, — under cover of
night. The right wing was instantly to seize
upon the penitentiary building, just converted
into an arsenal ; while the left wing was to take
possession of the powder-house. These two
columns were to be armed chiefly with clubs, as
their undertaking depended for success upon
surprise, and was expected to prevail without
hard fighting. But it was the central force,

armed with muskets, cutlasses, knives, and
pikes, upon which the chief responsibility
rested; these men were to enter the town at
both ends simultaneously, and begin a general
carnage, none being excepted save the French
inhabitants, who were supposed for some reason
to be friendly to the negroes. In a very few
hours, it was thought, they would have entire
control of the metropolis. And that this hope
was not in the least unreasonable, was shown
by the subsequent confessions of weakness from
the whites. "They could scarcely have failed
of success," wrote the Richmond correspondent of the Boston *Chronicle;* "for, after all,
we could only muster four or five hundred
men, of whom not more than thirty had
muskets."

For the insurgents, if successful, the penitentiary held several thousand stand of arms; the
powder-house was well stocked; the Capitol
contained the State treasury; the mills would
give them bread; the control of the bridge
across James River would keep off enemies
from beyond. Thus secured and provided,

they planned to issue proclamations summoning to their standard "their fellow-negroes and the friends of humanity throughout the continent." In a week, it was estimated, they would have fifty thousand men on their side, with which force they could easily possess themselves of other towns; and, indeed, a slave named John Scott — possibly the dangerous possessor of the ten dollars — was already appointed to head the attack on Petersburg. But in case of final failure, the project included a retreat to the mountains, with their new-found property. John Brown was therefore anticipated by Gabriel, sixty years before, in believing the Virginia mountains to have been '"created, from the foundation of the world, as a place of refuge for fugitive slaves."

These are the statements of the contemporary witnesses; they are repeated in many newspapers of the year 1800, and are in themselves clear and consistent. Whether they are on the whole exaggerated or under-stated, it is now impossible to say. It is certain that a Richmond paper of Sept. 12 (quoted in the

New-York *Gazette* of Sept. 18) declares that
"the plot has been entirely exploded, which
was shallow; and, had the attempt been made
to carry it into execution, but little resistance would have been required to render the
scheme entirely abortive." But it is necessary to remember that this is no more than
the Charleston newspapers said at the very
crisis of Denmark Vesey's formidable plot.
"Last evening," wrote a lady from Charleston
in 1822, "twenty-five hundred of our citizens
were under arms to guard our property and
lives. But it is a subject *not to be mentioned*
[so underscored]; and unless you hear of it
elsewhere, say nothing about it." Thus it is
always hard to know whether to assume the
facts of an insurrection as above or below
the estimates. This Virginian excitement also
happened at a period of intense political agitation, and was seized upon as a boon by the
Federalists. The very article above quoted is
ironically headed "Holy Insurrection," and
takes its motto from Jefferson, with profuse
capital letters: "The Spirit of the Master is

abating, that of the Slave rising from the dust, his condition mollifying."

In view of the political aspect thus given to the plot, and of its ingenuity and thoroughness likewise, the Virginians were naturally disposed to attribute to white men some share in it; and speculation presently began to run wild. The newspapers were soon full of theories, no two being alike, and no one credible. The plot originated, some said, in certain handbills written by Jefferson's friend Callender, then in prison at Richmond on a charge of sedition; these were circulated by two French negroes, aided by a "United Irishman" calling himself a Methodist preacher, and it was in consideration of these services that no Frenchman was to be injured by the slaves. When Gabriel was arrested, the editor of the *United-States Gazette* affected much diplomatic surprise that no letters were *yet* found upon his person "from Fries, Gallatin, or Duane, nor was he at the time of his capture accompanied by any United Irishman." "He, however, acknowledges that there are others concerned,

and that he is not the principal instigator."
All Federalists agreed that the Southern
Democratic talk was constructive insurrection,
— which it certainly was, — and they painted
graphic pictures of noisy "Jacobins" over
their wine, and eager dusky listeners behind
their chairs. "It is evident that the French
principles of liberty and equality have been
effused into the minds of the negroes, and
that the incautious and intemperate use of the
words by some whites among us have inspired
them with hopes of success." "While the fiery
Hotspurs of the State vociferate their *French
babble* of the natural equality of man, the
insulted negro will be constantly stimulated
to cast away his cords, and to sharpen his
pike." "It is, moreover, believed, though not
positively known, that a great many of our
profligate and abandoned whites (who are
distinguished by the burlesque appellation of
Democrats) are implicated with the blacks, and
would have joined them if they had commenced
their operations. . . . The Jacobin printers and
their friends are panic - struck. Never was

terror more strongly depicted in the countenances of men." These extracts from three different Federalist newspapers show the amiable emotions of that side of the house; while Democratic Duane, in the *Aurora*, could find no better repartee than to attribute the whole trouble to the policy of the administration in renewing commercial intercourse with San Domingo.

I have discovered in the Norfolk *Epitome of the Times*, for Oct. 9, 1800, a remarkable epistle written from Richmond Jail by the unfortunate Callender himself. He indignantly denies the charges against the Democrats, of complicity in dangerous plots, boldly retorting them upon the Federalists. "An insurrection at this critical moment by the negroes of the Southern States would have thrown every thing into confusion, and consequently it was to have prevented the choice of electors in the whole or the greater part of the States to the south of the Potomac. Such a disaster must have tended directly to injure the interests of Mr. Jefferson, and to promote the slender possibility

of a second election of Mr. Adams." And, to
be sure, the *United - States Gazette* followed
up the thing with a good, single-minded party
malice which cannot be surpassed in these
present days, ending in such altitudes of sub-
lime coolness as the following : " The insurrection of the negroes in the Southern States,
which appears to be organized on the true
French plan, must be decisive, with every
reflecting man in those States, of the election of
Mr. Adams and Gen. Pinckney. The military
skill and approved bravery of the general must
be peculiarly valuable to his countrymen at
these trying moments." Let us have a military
Vice-President, by all means, to meet this
formidable exigency of Gabriel's peck of bullets, and this unexplained three shillings in the
pocket of " Prosser's Ben " !

But Gabriel's campaign failed, like that of
the Federalists ; and the appointed day brought
disasters more fatal than even the sword of
Gen. Pinckney. The affrighted negroes declared that " the stars in their courses fought
against Sisera." The most furious tempest ever

known in Virginia burst upon the land that day,
instead of an insurrection. Roads and plantations were submerged. Bridges were carried
away. The fords, which then, as now, were
the frequent substitutes for bridges in that
region, were rendered wholly impassable. The
Brook Swamp, one of the most important stra-
tegic points of the insurgents, was entirely
inundated, hopelessly dividing Prosser's farm
from Richmond; the country negroes could not
get in, nor those from the city get out. The
thousand men dwindled to a few hundred, and
these half paralyzed by superstition ; there was
nothing to do but to dismiss them, and before
they could re-assemble they were betrayed.

That the greatest alarm was instantly created
throughout the community, there is no question. All the city of Richmond was in arms,
and in all large towns of the State the night-
patrol was doubled. It is a little amusing to
find it formally announced, that "the Governor,
impressed with the magnitude of the danger,
has appointed for himself three aides-de-camp."
A troop of United-States cavalry was ordered

to Richmond. Numerous arrests were made. Men were convicted on one day, and hanged on the next, — five, six, ten, fifteen at a time, almost without evidence. Three hundred dollars were offered by Gov. Monroe for the arrest of Gabriel; as much more for another chief named Jack Bowler, *alias* Ditcher; whereupon Bowler *alias* Ditcher surrendered himself, but it took some weeks to get upon the track of Gabriel. He was finally captured at Norfolk, on board a schooner just arrived from Richmond, in whose hold he had concealed himself for eleven days, having thrown overboard a bayonet and bludgeon, which were his only arms. Crowds of people collected to see him, including many of his own color. He was arrested on Sept. 24, convicted on Oct. 3, and executed on Oct. 7; and it is known of him further, only, that, like almost all leaders of slave insurrections, he showed a courage which his enemies could not gainsay. "When he was apprehended, he manifested the greatest marks of firmness and confidence, showing not the least disposition to equivocate, or screen himself from justice," — but making no confession that could implicate any one else. " The behavior of Gabriel under his misfortunes," said the Norfolk *Epitome* of Sept. 25, "was such as might be expected from a mind capable of forming the daring project which he had conceived." The *United-States Gazette* for Oct. 9 states, more sarcastically, that " the general is said to have manifested the utmost composure, and with the true spirit of heroism seems ready to resign his high office, and even his life, rather than gratify the officious inquiries of the Governor."

Some of these newspapers suggest that the authorities found it good policy to omit the statement made by Gabriel, whatever it was. At any rate, he assured them that he was by no means the sole instigator of the affair ; he could name many, even in Norfolk, who were more deeply concerned. To his brother Solomon he is said to have stated that the real head of the plot was Jack Bowler. Still another leader was " Gen. John Scott," already mentioned, the slave of Mr. Greenhow, hired by Mr. McCrea.

IIe was captured by his employer in Norfolk,
just as he was boldly entering a public convey-
ance to escape; and the Baltimore *Telegraphe*
declared that he had a written paper directing
him to apply to Alexander Biddenhurst or
Weddenhurst in Philadelphia, "corner of Coats
Alley and Budd Street, who would supply
his needs." What became of this military
individual, or of his Philadelphia sympathizers,
does not appear. But it was noticed, as
usually happens in such cases, that all the insurgents had previously passed for saints. "It
consists within my knowledge," says one letter-
writer, "that many of these wretches who were or
would have been partakers in the plot have been
treated with the utmost tenderness by their masters, and were more like children than slaves."

These appear to be all the details now accessible of this once famous plot. They were not
very freely published, even at the time. "The
minutiæ of the conspiracy have not been
detailed to the public," said the Salem (Mass.)
Gazette of Oct. 7, "and perhaps, through a
mistaken notion of prudence and policy, will

not be detailed in the Richmond papers." The New - York *Commercial Advertiser* of Oct. 13 was still more explicit. "The trials of the negroes concerned in the late insurrection are suspended until the opinions of the Legislature can be had on the subject. This measure is said to be owing to the immense numbers who are interested in the plot, whose death, should they all be found guilty and be executed, will nearly produce the annihilation of the blacks in this part of the country." And in the next issue of the same journal a Richmond correspondent makes a similar statement, with the following addition: "A conditional amnesty is perhaps expected. At the next session of the Legislature [of Virginia], they took into consideration the subject referred to them, in secret session, with closed doors. The whole result of their deliberations has never yet been made public, as the injunction of secrecy has never been removed. To satisfy the court, the public, and themselves, they had a task so difficult to perform, that it is not surprising that their deliberations were in secret."

It is a matter of historical interest to know that in these mysterious sessions lay the germs of the American Colonization Society. A correspondence was at once secretly commenced between the Governor of Virginia and the President of the United States, with a view to securing a grant of land whither troublesome slaves might be banished. Nothing came of it then; but in 1801, 1802, and 1804, these attempts were renewed. And finally, on Jan. 22, 1805, the following vote was passed, still in secret session: "*Resolved*, that the Senators of this State in the Congress of the United States be instructed, and the Representatives be requested, to use their best efforts for the obtaining from the General Government a competent portion of territory in the State of Louisiana, to be appropriated to the residence of such people of color as have been or shall be emancipated, or hereafter may become dangerous to the public safety," etc. But of all these efforts nothing was known till their record was accidentally discovered by Charles Fenton Mercer in 1816. He at once brought the mat-

ter to light, and moved a similar resolution in
the Virginia Legislature; it was almost unanimously adopted, and the first formal meeting
of the Colonization Society, in 1817, was called
" in aid " of this Virginia movement.   But the
whole correspondence was never made public
until the Nat Turner insurrection of 1831
recalled the previous excitement; and these
papers were demanded by Mr. Summers, a
member of the Legislature, who described them
as " having originated in a convulsion similar to
that which had recently, but more terribly,
occurred."

But neither these subsequent papers, nor any
documents which now appear accessible, can
supply any authentic or trustworthy evidence
as to the real extent of the earlier plot.   It
certainly was not confined to the mere envi-
rons of Richmond.   The Norfolk *Epitome* of
Oct. 6 states that on the 6th and 7th of the
previous month one hundred and fifty blacks,
including twenty from Norfolk, were assembled near Whitlock's Mills in Suffolk County,
and remained in the neighborhood till the

failure of the Richmond plan became known.
Petersburg newspapers also had letters containing similar tales. Then the alarm spread
more widely. Near Edenton, N.C., there
was undoubtedly a real insurrection, though
promptly suppressed; and many families ultimately removed from that vicinity in consequence. In Charleston, S.C., there was still
greater excitement, if the contemporary press
may be trusted; it was reported that the freeholders had been summoned to appear in arms,
on penalty of a fine of fifteen pounds, which
many preferred to pay rather than risk taking
the fever which then prevailed. These reports
were, however, zealously contradicted in letters
from Charleston, dated Oct. 8; and the Charleston newspapers up to Sept. 17 had certainly
contained no reference to any especial excitement. This alone might not settle the fact, for
reasons already given. But the omission of any
such affair from the valuable pamphlet published in 1822 by Edwin C. Holland, containing reminiscences of insurrections in South
Carolina, is presumptive evidence that no very
extended agitation occurred.

But wherever there was a black population, slave or emancipated, men's startled consciences made cowards of them all, and recognized the negro as a dangerous man, because an injured one. In Philadelphia it was seriously proposed to prohibit the use of sky-rockets for a time, because they had been employed as signals in San Domingo. "Even in Boston," said the New-York *Daily Advertiser* of Sept. 20, "fears are expressed, and measures of prevention adopted." This probably refers to a singular advertisement which appeared in some of the Boston newspapers on Sept. 16, and runs as follows : —

" NOTICE TO BLACKS.

" The officers of the police having made returns to the subscriber of the names of the following persons who are Africans or negroes, not subjects of the Emperor of Morocco nor citizens of any of the United States, the same are hereby warned and directed to depart out of this Commonwealth before the tenth day of October next, as they would avoid the pains and penalties of the law in that case provided, which was passed by the Legislature March 26, 1788.

"CHARLES BULFINCH, Superintendent.

" By order and direction of the Selectmen."

The names annexed are about three hundred, with the places of their supposed origin, and they occupy a column of the paper. So at least asserts the *United-States Gazette* of Sept. 23. "It seems probable," adds the editor, "from the nature of the notice, that some suspicion of the design of the negroes is entertained; and we regret to say there is too much cause." The law of 1788 above mentioned was "An Act for suppressing rogues, vagabonds, and the like," which forbade all persons of African descent, unless citizens of some one of the United States or subjects of the Emperor of Morocco, from remaining more than two months within the Commonwealth, on penalty of imprisonment and hard labor. This singular statute remained unrepealed until 1834.

Amid the general harmony in the contemporary narratives of Gabriel's insurrection, it would be improper to pass by one exceptional legend, which by some singular fatality has obtained more circulation than all the true accounts put together. I can trace it no farther back than Nat Turner's time, when it was published in the Albany *Evening Journal;* thence transferred to the *Liberator* of Sept. 17, 1831, and many other newspapers; then refuted in detail by the *Richmond Enquirer* of Oct. 21; then resuscitated in the John-Brown epoch by the Philadelphia *Press,* and extensively copied. It is fresh, spirited, and full of graphic and interesting details, nearly every one of which is altogether false.

Gabriel in this narrative becomes a rather mythical being, of vast abilities and life-long preparations. He bought his freedom, it is stated, at the age of twenty-one, and then travelled all over the Southern States, enlisting confederates and forming stores of arms. At length his plot was discovered, in consequence of three negroes having been seen riding out of a stable-yard together; and the Governor offered a reward of ten thousand dollars for further information, to which a Richmond gentleman added as much more. Gabriel concealed himself on board the "Sally Ann," a vessel just sailing for San Domingo, and was revealed by his little nephew, whom he had sent for a jug of rum. Finally, the narrative puts an eloquent dying speech into Gabriel's mouth, and, to give a properly tragic consummation, causes him to be torn to death by four wild horses. The last item is, however, omitted in the more recent reprints of the story.

Every one of these statements appears to be absolutely erroneous. Gabriel lived and died a slave, and was probably never out of Virginia. His plot was voluntarily revealed by accomplices. The rewards offered for his arrest amounted to three hundred dollars only. He concealed himself on board the schooner "Mary," bound to Norfolk, and was discovered by the police. He died on the gallows, with ten associates, having made no address to the court or the people. All the errors of the statement were contradicted when it was first made public, but they have proved very hard to kill.

Some of these events were embodied in a song bearing the same title with this essay, "Gabriel's Defeat," and set to a tune of the same name, both being composed by a colored

man. Several witnesses have assured me of
having heard this sung in Virginia, as a favorite
air at the dances of the white people, as well
as in the huts of the slaves. It is surely one
of history's strange parallelisms, that this fatal
enterprise, like that of John Brown afterwards,
should thus have embalmed itself in music.
And twenty-two years after these events, their
impression still remained vivid enough for
Benjamin Lundy, in Tennessee, to write: "So
well had they matured their plot, and so com-
pletely had they organized their system of
operations, that nothing but a seemingly mirac-
ulous intervention of the arm of Providence
was supposed to have been capable of saving
the city from pillage and flames, and the inhabitants thereof from butchery. So dreadful was
the alarm and so great the consternation produced on this occasion, that a member of Congress from that State was some time after heard
to express himself in his place as follows:
'The night-bell is never heard to toll in the
city of Richmond, but the anxious mother

presses her infant more closely to her bosom.' "
The Congressman was John Randolph of Roa-
noke, and it was Gabriel who had taught him
the lesson.

And longer than the melancholy life of that
wayward statesman, — down even to the beginning of the American civil war, — there lin-
gered in Richmond a memorial of those days,
most peculiar and most instructive.   Before the
days of secession, when the Northern traveller in
Virginia, after traversing for weary leagues its
miry ways, its desolate fields, and its flowery
forests, rode at last into its metropolis, he was
sure to be guided ere long to visit its stately
Capitol, modelled by Jefferson, when French
minister, from the Maison Carrée.   Standing
before it, he might admire undisturbed the
Grecian outline of its exterior; but he found
himself forbidden to enter, save by passing an
armed and uniformed sentinel at the doorway.
No other State of the Union then found it
necessary to protect its State House by a permanent cordon of bayonets.   Yet there for half

a century stood sentinel the "Public Guard" of Virginia; and when the traveller asked the origin of the precaution, he was told that it was the lasting memorial of Gabriel's Defeat.

DENMARK VESEY

O N Saturday afternoon, May 25, 1822, a
slave named Devany, belonging to Col.
Prioleau of Charleston, S.C., was sent to
market by his mistress, — the colonel being
absent in the country. After doing his errands,
he strolled down upon the wharves in the
enjoyment of that magnificent wealth of lei-
sure which usually characterized the former
"house-servant" of the South, when beyond
hail of the street-door. He presently noticed a
small vessel lying in the stream, with a peculiar
flag flying; and while looking at it, he was
accosted by a slave named William, belonging
to Mr. John Paul, who remarked to him, "I
have often seen a flag with the number 76,
but never one with the number 96 upon it before." After some further conversation on this
trifling point, William suddenly inquired, "Do

you know that something serious is about to take place?" Devany disclaiming the knowledge of any graver impending crisis than the family dinner, the other went on to inform him that many of the slaves were "determined to right themselves." "We are determined," he added, "to shake off our bondage, and for that purpose we stand on a good foundation; many have joined, and if you will go with me, I will show you the man who has the list of names, and who will take yours down."

This startling disclosure was quite too much for Devany: he was made of the wrong material for so daring a project; his genius was culinary, not revolutionary. Giving some excuse for breaking off the conversation, he went forthwith to consult a free colored man, named Pensil or Pencell, who advised him to warn his master instantly. So he lost no time in telling the secret to his mistress and her young son; and on the return of Col. Prioleau from the country, five days afterward, it was at once revealed to him. Within an hour or two he stated the facts to Mr. Hamilton, the intendant, or, as he would now be called, mayor; Mr. Hamilton at once summoned the corporation, and by five o'clock Devany and William were under examination.

This was the first warning of a plot which ultimately filled Charleston with terror. And yet so thorough and so secret was the organization of the negroes, that a fortnight passed without yielding the slightest information beyond the very little which was obtained from these two. William Paul was, indeed, put in confinement, and soon gave evidence inculpating two slaves as his employers, — Mingo Harth and Peter Poyas. But these men, when arrested, behaved with such perfect coolness, and treated the charge with such entire levity; — their trunks and premises, when searched, were so innocent of all alarming contents; — that they were soon discharged by the wardens. William Paul at length became alarmed for his own safety, and began to let out further facts piecemeal, and to inculpate other men. But some of those very men came voluntarily to the intendant, on hearing that they were suspected, and indignantly offered themselves for examination. Puzzled and bewildered, the municipal government kept the thing as secret as possible, placed the city guard in an efficient condition, provided sixteen hundred rounds of ball cartridges, and ordered the sentinels and patrols to be armed with loaded muskets. "Such had been our fancied security, that the guard had previously gone on duty without muskets, and with only sheathed bayonets and bludgeons."

It has since been asserted, though perhaps on questionable authority, that the Secretary of War was informed of the plot, even including some details of the plan and the leader's name, before it was known in Charleston. If so, he utterly disregarded it; and, indeed, so well did the negroes play their part, that the whole report was eventually disbelieved, while — as was afterwards proved — they went on to complete their secret organization, and hastened by a fortnight the appointed day of attack. Unfortunately for their plans, however, another betrayal took place at the very last moment,

from a different direction. A class-leader in a
Methodist church had been persuaded or bribed
by his master to procure further disclosures.
He at length came and stated, that, about
three months before, a man named Rolla,
slave of Gov. Bennett, had communicated to
a friend of his the fact of an intended insurrection, and had said that the time fixed for
the outbreak was the following Sunday night,
June 16. As this conversation took place on
Friday, it gave but a very short time for the
city authorities to act, especially as they wished
neither to endanger the city nor to alarm it.

Yet so cautiously was the game played on
both sides that the whole thing was still kept
a secret from the Charleston public ; and some
members of the city government did not fully
appreciate their danger till they had passed it.
" The whole was concealed," wrote the governor
afterwards, " until the time came ; but secret
preparations were made. Saturday night and
Sunday morning passed without demonstra-
tions ; doubts were excited, and counter orders
issued for diminishing the guard." It after-

wards proved that these preparations showed
to the slaves that their plot was betrayed, and
so saved the city without public alarm. Newspaper correspondence soon was full of the
story, each informant of course hinting plainly
that he had been behind the scenes all along,
and had withheld it only to gratify the authorities in their policy of silence. It was " now
no longer a secret," they wrote ; adding, that,
for five or six weeks, but little attention had
been paid by the community to these rumors,
the city council having kept it carefully to
themselves until a number of suspicious slaves
had been arrested. This refers to ten prisoners
who were seized on June 18, an arrest which
killed the plot, and left only the terrors of
what might have been. The investigation,
thus publicly commenced, soon revealed a free
colored man named Denmark Vesey as the
leader of the enterprise, — among his chief
coadjutors being that innocent Peter and that
unsuspecting Mingo who had been examined
and discharged nearly three weeks before.

It is matter of demonstration, that, but for

the military preparations on the appointed
Sunday night, the attempt would have been
made. The ringleaders had actually met for
their final arrangements, when, by comparing
notes, they found themselves foiled; and within
another week they were prisoners on trial.
Nevertheless, the plot which they had laid was
the most elaborate insurrectionary project ever
formed by American slaves, and came the nearest to a terrible success. In boldness of con-
ception and thoroughness of organization there
has been nothing to compare with it; and it is
worth while to dwell somewhat upon its details,
first introducing the *dramatis personæ*.

Denmark Vesey had come very near figuring
as a revolutionist in Hayti, instead of South
Carolina. Capt. Vesey, an old resident of
Charleston, commanded a ship that traded
between St. Thomas and Cape Français, during
our Revolutionary War, in the slave-transporta-
tion line. In the year 1781 he took on board a
cargo of three hundred and ninety slaves, and
sailed for the Cape. On the passage, he and
his officers were much attracted by the beauty

and intelligence of a boy of fourteen, whom they unanimously adopted into the cabin as a pet. They gave him new clothes, and a new name, Télémaque, which was afterwards gradually corrupted into Telmak and Denmark. They amused themselves with him until their arrival at Cape Français, and then, " having no use for the boy," sold their pet as if he had been a macaw or a monkey. Capt. Vesey sailed for St. Thomas; and, presently making another trip to Cape Français, was surprised to hear from his consignee that Télémaque would be returned on his hands as being " unsound," — not in theology nor in morals, but in body, — subject to epileptic fits, in fact. According to the custom of that place, the boy was examined by the city physician, who required Capt. Vesey to take him back; and Denmark served him faithfully, with no trouble from epilepsy, for twenty years, travelling all over the world with him, and learning to speak various languages. In 1800 he drew a prize of fifteen hundred dollars in the East Bay-street Lottery, with which he bought his freedom

from his master for six hundred dollars, —
much less than his market value. From that
time, the official report says, he worked as a
carpenter in Charleston, distinguished for physi-
cal strength and energy. " Among those of his
color he was looked up to with awe and respect.
His temper was impetuous and domineering in
the extreme, qualifying him for the despotic
rule of which he was ambitious. All his passions were ungovernable and savage ; and to
his numerous wives and children he displayed
the haughty and capricious cruelty of an Eastern bashaw."

" For several years before he disclosed his
intentions to any one, he appears to have been
constantly and assiduously engaged in endeav-
oring to imbitter the minds of the colored population against the white. He rendered himself
perfectly familiar with all those parts of the
Scriptures which he thought he could pervert
to his purpose, and would readily quote them
to prove that slavery was contrary to the
laws of God ; that slaves were bound to
attempt their emancipation, however shocking

and bloody might be the consequences; and
that such efforts would not only be pleasing
to the Almighty, but were absolutely enjoined,
and their success predicted, in the Scriptures.
His favorite texts when he addressed those of
his own color were Zech. xiv. 1–3, and Josh.
vi. 21; and in all his conversations he identi-
fied their situation with that of the Israelites.
The number of inflammatory pamphlets on
slavery brought into Charleston from some of
our sister States within the last four years
(and once from Sierra Leone), and distributed
amongst the colored population of the city,
for which there was a great facility, in consequence of the unrestricted intercourse allowed
to persons of color between the different States
in the Union, and the speeches in Congress
of those opposed to the admission of Missouri
into the Union, perhaps garbled and misrepre-
sented, furnished him with ample means for
inflaming the minds of the colored population
of the State; and by distorting certain parts
of those speeches, or selecting from them
particular passages, he persuaded but too many

that Congress had actually declared them free,
and that they were held in bondage contrary
to the laws of the land. Even whilst walking
through the streets in company with another,
he was not idle; for if his companion bowed
to a white person, he would rebuke him, and
observe that all men were born equal, and that
he was surprised that any one would degrade
himself by such conduct; that he would never
cringe to the whites, nor ought any one who
had the feelings of a man. When answered,
'We are slaves,' he would sarcastically and
indignantly reply, 'You deserve to remain
slaves;' and if he were further asked, 'What
can we do?' he would remark, 'Go and buy a
spelling-book, and read the fable of Hercules
and the Wagoner,' which he would then repeat,
and apply it to their situation. He also sought
every opportunity of entering into conversation with white persons, when they could be
overheard by negroes near by, especially in
grog-shops, — during which conversation he
would artfully introduce some bold remark on
slavery ; and sometimes, when, from the char-

acter he was conversing with, he found he
might still be bolder, he would go so far, that,
had not his declarations in such situations been
clearly proved, they would scarcely have been
credited. He continued this course until some
time after the commencement of the last
winter ; by which time he had not only
obtained incredible influence amongst persons
of color, but many feared him more than their
owners, and, one of them declared, even more
than his God."

It was proved against him, that his house
had been the principal place of meeting for
the conspirators, that all the others habitually
referred to him as the leader, and that he had
shown great address in dealing with different
temperaments and overcoming a variety of
scruples. One witness testified that Vesey had
read to him from the Bible about the deliverance of the children of Israel; another, that
he had read to him a speech which had been
delivered " in Congress by a Mr. King " on the
subject of slavery, and Vesey had said that
" this Mr. King was the black man's friend ;

that he, Mr. King, had declared he would con-
tinue to speak, write, and publish pamphlets
against slavery the longest day he lived, until
the Southern States consented to emancipate
their slaves, for that slavery was a great disgrace to the country." But among all the
reports there are only two sentences which
really reveal the secret soul of Denmark Vesey,
and show his impulses and motives. "He said
he did not go with Creighton to Africa, because
he had not a will; he wanted to stay and see
what he could do for his fellow-creatures."
The other takes us still nearer home. Monday
Gell stated in his confession, that Vesey, on
first broaching the plan to him, said "he was
satisfied with his own condition, being free;
but, as all his children were slaves, he wished
to see what could be done for them."

It is strange to turn from this simple statement of a perhaps intelligent preference, on
the part of a parent, for seeing his offspring in
a condition of freedom, to the *naïve* astonishment of his judges. "It is difficult to imagine,"
says the sentence finally passed on Denmark

Vesey, " what infatuation could have prompted
you to attempt an enterprise so wild and
visionary.   You were a free man, comparatively
wealthy, and enjoyed every comfort compatible
with your situation.   You had, therefore, much
to risk and little to gain."   Yet one witness
testified: " Vesey said the negroes were living
such an abominable life, they ought to rise.
I said, I was living well; he said, though I was,
others were not, and that 'twas such fools as
I that were in the way and would not help
them, and that after all things were well he
would mark me."   " His general conversation,"
said another witness, a white boy, " was about
religion, which he would apply to slavery; as,
for instance, he would speak of the creation
of the world, in which he would say all men
had equal rights, blacks as well as whites, etc.;
all his religious remarks were mingled with
slavery."   And the firmness of this purpose
did not leave him, even after the betrayal of
his cherished plans.   " After the plot was discovered," said Monday Gell, in his confession,
" Vesey said it was all over, unless an attempt

were made to rescue those who might be condemned, by rushing on the people and saving the prisoners, or all dying together."

The only person to divide with Vesey the claim of leadership was Peter Poyas. Vesey was the missionary of the cause, but Peter was the organizing mind. He kept the register of "candidates," and decided who should or should not be enrolled. "We can't live so," he often reminded his confederates; "we must break the yoke." "God has a hand in it; we have been meeting for four years, and are not yet betrayed." Peter was a ship-carpenter, and a slave of great value. He was to be the military leader. His plans showed some natural generalship: he arranged the night-attack; he planned the enrolment of a mounted troop to scour the streets; and he had a list of all the shops where arms and ammunition were kept for sale. He voluntarily undertook the management of the most difficult part of the enterprise, — the capture of the main guard-house, — and had pledged himself to advance alone and surprise the sentinel. He was said to have a magnetism in his eyes, of which his confederates stood in great awe; if he once got his eye upon a man, there was no resisting it. A white witness has since narrated, that, after his arrest, he was chained to the floor in a cell, with another of the conspirators. Men in authority came, and sought by promises, threats, and even tortures, to ascertain the names of other accomplices. His companion, wearied out with pain and suffering, and stimulated by the hope of saving his own life, at last began to yield. Peter raised himself, leaned upon his elbow, looked at the poor fellow, saying quietly, "Die like a man," and instantly lay down again. It was enough; not another word was extorted.

One of the most notable individuals in the plot was a certain Jack Purcell, commonly called Gullah Jack, — Gullah signifying Angola, the place of his origin. A conjurer by profession and by lineal heritage in his own country, he had resumed the practice of his vocation on this side the Atlantic. For fifteen years he had wielded in secret an immense influence among a sable constituency in Charleston; and as he had the reputation of being invulnerable, and of teaching invulnerability as an art, he was very good at beating up recruits for insurrection. Over those of Angolese descent, especially, he was a perfect king, and made them join in the revolt as one man. They met him monthly at a place called Bulkley's Farm, selected because the black overseer on that plantation was one of the initiated, and because the farm was accessible by water, thus enabling them to elude the patrol. There they prepared cartridges and pikes, and had primitive banquets, which assumed a melodramatic character under the inspiriting guidance of Jack. If a fowl was privately roasted, that mystic individual muttered incantations over it; and then they all grasped at it, exclaiming, "Thus we pull Buckra to pieces!" He gave them parched corn and ground-nuts to be eaten as internal safeguards on the day before the outbreak, and a consecrated *cullah*, or crab's claw, to be carried in the mouth by each, as an amulet. These rather questionable means secured him a power which was very unquestionable; the witnesses examined in his presence all showed dread of his conjurations, and referred to him indirectly, with a kind of awe, as "the little man who can't be shot."

When Gullah Jack was otherwise engaged, there seems to have been a sort of deputy seer employed in the enterprise, a blind man named Philip. He was a preacher; was said to have been born with a caul on his head, and so claimed the gift of second-sight. Timid adherents were brought to his house for ghostly counsel. "Why do you look so timorous?" he said to William Garner, and then quoted Scripture, "Let not your heart be troubled." That a blind man should know how he looked, was beyond the philosophy of the visitor; and this piece of rather cheap ingenuity carried the day.

Other leaders were appointed also. Monday Gell was the scribe of the enterprise; he was a native African, who had learned to read and write. He was by trade a harness-maker, working chiefly on his own account. He confessed

that he had written a letter to President Boyer
of the new black republic; "the letter was
about the sufferings of the blacks, and to know
if the people of St. Domingo would help them
if they made an effort to free themselves."
This epistle was sent by the black cook of
a Northern schooner, and the envelope was
addressed to a relative of the bearer.

Tom Russell was the armorer, and made
pikes "on a very improved model," the official
report admits. Polydore Faber fitted the
weapons with handles. Bacchus Hammett had
charge of the fire-arms and ammunition, not as
yet a laborious duty. William Garner and
Mingo Harth were to lead the horse-company.
Lot Forrester was the courier, and had done,
no one ever knew how much, in the way of
enlisting country negroes, of whom Ned
Bennett was to take command when enlisted.
Being the governor's servant, Ned was probably credited with some official experience.
These were the officers: now for the plan of
attack.

It was the custom then, as later, for the

country negroes to flock largely into Charleston on Sunday. More than a thousand came, on ordinary occasions, and a far larger number might at any time make their appearance without exciting any suspicion. They gathered in, especially by water, from the opposite sides of Ashley and Cooper Rivers, and from the neighboring islands; and they came in a great number of canoes of various sizes, — many of which could carry a hundred men, — which were ordinarily employed in bringing agricultural products to the Charleston market. To get an approximate knowledge of the number, the city government once ordered the persons thus arriving to be counted, — and that during the progress of the trials, at a time when the negroes were rather fearful of coming into town; and it was found, that, even then, there were more than five hundred visitors on a single Sunday. This fact, then, was the essential point in the plan of insurrection. Whole plantations were found to have been enlisted among the "candidates," as they were termed; and it was proved that the city negroes, who lived nearest the place of meeting, had agreed to conceal these confederates in their houses to a large extent, on the night of the proposed outbreak.

The details of the plan, however, were not rashly committed to the mass of the confederates; they were known only to a few, and were finally to be announced only after the evening prayer-meetings on the appointed Sunday. But each leader had his own company enlisted, and his own work marked out. When the clock struck twelve, all were to move. Peter Poyas was to lead a party ordered to assemble at South Bay, and to be joined by a force from James's Island; he was then to march up and seize the arsenal and guard-house opposite St. Michael's Church, and detach a sufficient number to cut off all white citizens who should appear at the alarm-posts. A second body of negroes, from the country and the Neck, headed by Ned Bennett, was to assemble on the Neck, and seize the arsenal there. A third was to meet at Gov. Bennett's Mills, under command of Rolla, and, after putting the governor and intendant to death, to march through the city,

or be posted at Cannon's Bridge, thus preventing the inhabitants of Cannonsborough from
entering the city. A fourth, partly from the
country, and partly from the neighboring local-
ities in the city, was to rendezvous on Gadsden's
Wharf, and attack the upper guard-house.
A fifth, composed of country and Neck negroes,
was to assemble at Bulkley's Farm, two miles
and a half from the city, seize the upper powder-
magazine, and then march down; and a sixth
was to assemble at Denmark Vesey's, and obey
his orders. A seventh detachment, under
Gullah Jack, was to assemble in Boundary
Street, at the head of King Street, to capture
the arms of the Neck company of militia, and
to take an additional supply from Mr. Duquercron's shop. The naval stores on Mey's Wharf
were also to be attacked. Meanwhile, a horse-
company, consisting of many draymen, hostlers,
and butcher-boys, was to meet at Lightwood's
Alley, and then scour the streets to prevent
the whites from assembling. Every white man
coming out of his own door was to be killed;
and, if necessary, the city was to be fired in

several places, — slow-match for this purpose
having been purloined from the public arsenal,
and placed in an accessible position.

Beyond this, the plan of action was either
unformed or undiscovered; some slight reliance
seems to have been placed on English aid, —
more on assistance from St. Domingo. At any
rate, all the ships in the harbor were to be
seized; and in these, if the worst came to the
worst, those most deeply inculpated could set
sail, bearing with them, perhaps, the spoils of
shops and of banks. It seems to be admitted by
the official narrative, that they might have been
able, at that season of the year, and with the
aid of the fortifications on the Neck and around
the harbor, to retain possession of the city for
some time.

So unsuspicious were the authorities, so un-
prepared the citizens, so open to attack lay the
city, that nothing seemed necessary to the success of the insurgents except organization and
arms. Indeed, the plan of organization easily
covered a supply of arms. By their own con-
tributions they had secured enough to strike

the first blow, — a few hundred pikes and daggers, together with swords and guns for the leaders. But they had carefully marked every place in the city where weapons were to be obtained. On King-street Road, beyond the municipal limits, in a common wooden shop, were left unguarded the arms of the Neck company of militia, to the number of several hundred stand; and these were to be secured by Bacchus Hammett, whose master kept the establishment. In Mr. Duquercron's shop there were deposited for sale as many more weapons; and they had noted Mr. Schirer's shop in Queen Street, and other gunsmiths' establishments. Finally, the State arsenal in Meeting Street, a building with no defences except ordinary wooden doors, was to be seized early in the outbreak. Provided, therefore, that the first moves proved successful, all the rest appeared sure.

Very little seems to have been said among the conspirators in regard to any plans of riot or debauchery, subsequent to the capture of the city. Either their imaginations did not

dwell on them, or the witnesses did not dare
to give testimony, or the authorities to print
it. Death was to be dealt out, comprehensive
and terrible; but nothing more is mentioned.
One prisoner, Rolla, is reported in the evidence
to have dropped hints in regard to the destiny
of the women; and there was a rumor in the
newspapers of the time, that he or some other
of Gov. Bennett's slaves was to have taken
the governor's daughter, a young girl of sixteen, for his wife, in the event of success; but
this is all.   On the other hand, Denmark
Vesey was known to be for a war of immediate and total extermination; and when some
of the company opposed killing " the ministers
and the women and children," Vesey read from
the Scriptures that all should be cut off, and
said that "it was for their safety not to leave
one white skin alive, for this was the plan they
pursued at St. Domingo."   And all this was
not a mere dream of one lonely enthusiast, but
a measure which had been maturing for four
full years among several confederates, and had
been under discussion for five months among
multitudes of initiated " candidates."

As usual with slave-insurrections, the best men and those most trusted were deepest in the plot. Rolla was the only prominent' conspirator who was not an active church-member. " Most of the ringleaders," says a Charleston letter-writer of that day, " were the rulers or class-leaders in what is called the African Society, and were considered faithful, honest fellows. Indeed, many of the owners could not be convinced, till the fellows confessed themselves, that they were concerned, and that the first object of all was to kill their masters." And the first official report declares that it would not be difficult to assign a motive for the insurrectionists, " if it had not been distinctly proved, that, with scarcely an exception, they had no individual hardship to complain of, and were among the most humanely treated negroes in the city. The facilities for combining and confederating in such a scheme were amply afforded by the extreme indulgence and kindness which characterize the domestic treatment of our slaves. Many slave-owners among us, not satisfied with ministering to the wants of their domestics by all the comforts of abundant food and excellent clothing, with a misguided benevolence have not only permitted their instruction, but lent to such efforts their approbation and applause."

" I sympathize most sincerely," says the anonymous author of a pamphlet of the period, " with the very respectable and pious clergyman whose heart must still bleed at the recolletion that his confidential class-leader, but a week or two before his just conviction, had received the communion of the Lord's Supper from his hand. This wretch had been brought up in his pastor's family, and was treated with the same Christian attention as was shown to their own children." " To us who are accustomed to the base and proverbial ingratitude of these people, this ill return of kindness and confidence is not surprising; but they who are ignorant of their real character will read and wonder."

One demonstration of this " Christian attention " had lately been the closing of the African Church, — of which, as has been stated, most

of the leading revolutionists were members, —
on the ground that it tended to spread the
dangerous infection of the alphabet. On Jan.
15, 1821, the city marshal, John J. Lafar, had
notified " ministers of the gospel and others
who keep night- and Sunday-schools for slaves,
that the education of such persons is forbidden
by law, and that the city government feel
imperiously bound to enforce the penalty."
So that there were some special as well as
general grounds for disaffection among these
ungrateful favorites of fortune, the slaves.
Then there were fancied dangers. An absurd
report had somehow arisen, — since you cannot
keep men ignorant without making them unreasonable also, — that on the ensuing Fourth
of July the whites were to create a false alarm,
and that every black man coming out was to
be killed, " in order to thin them ; " this being
done to prevent their joining an imaginary
army supposed to be on its way from Hayti.
Others were led to suppose that Congress had
ended the Missouri Compromise discussion by
making them all free, and that the law would

protect their liberty if they could only secure
it. Others, again, were threatened with the
vengeance of the conspirators, unless they also
joined; on the night of attack, it was said, the
initiated would have a countersign, and all who
did not know it would share the fate of the
whites. Add to this the reading of Congressional speeches, and of the copious magazine of
revolution to be found in the Bible, — and it
was no wonder, if they for the first time were
roused, under the energetic leadership of Vesey,
to a full consciousness of their own condition.

"Not only were the leaders of good character,
and very much indulged by their owners; but
this was very generally the case with all who
were convicted, — many of them possessing the
highest confidence of their owners, and not one
of bad character." In one case it was proved
that Vesey had forbidden his followers to trust
a certain man, because he had once been seen
intoxicated. In another case it was shown
that a slave named George had made every
effort to obtain their confidence, but was constantly excluded from their meetings as a

talkative fellow who could not be trusted, —
a policy which his levity of manner, when
examined in court, fully justified. They took
no women into counsel, — not from any dis-
trust apparently, but in order that their children
might not be left uncared-for in case of defeat
and destruction. House-servants were rarely
trusted, or only when they had been carefully
sounded by the chief leaders. Peter Poyas, in
commissioning an agent to enlist men, gave
him excellent cautions: " Don't mention it to
those waiting-men who receive presents of old
coats, etc., from their masters, or they'll betray
us ; I will speak to them." When he did
speak, if he did not convince them, he at least
frightened them. But the chief reliance was
on those slaves who were hired out, and therefore more uncontrolled, — and also upon the
country negroes.

The same far-sighted policy directed the
conspirators to disarm suspicion by peculiarly
obedient and orderly conduct. And it shows
the precaution with which the thing was
carried on, that, although Peter Poyas was

proved to have had a list of some six hundred
persons, yet not one of his particular company
was ever brought to trial. As each leader
kept to himself the names of his proselytes,
and as Monday Gell was the only one of these
leaders who turned traitor, any opinion as to
the numbers actually engaged must be altogether conjectural. One witness said nine
thousand ; another, six thousand six hundred.
These statements were probably extravagant,
though not more so than Gov. Bennett's asser-
tion, on the other side, that "all who were
actually concerned had been brought to justice," — unless by this phrase he designates
only the ringleaders. The avowed aim of
the governor's letter, indeed, is to smooth the
thing over, for the credit and safety of the
city ; and its evasive tone contrasts strongly
with the more frank and thorough statements
of the judges, made after the thing could no
longer be hushed up. These high authorities
explicitly acknowledge that they had failed to
detect more than a small minority of those
concerned in the project, and seem to admit,

that, if it had once been brought to a head, the slaves generally would have joined in.

"We cannot venture to say," says the intendant's pamphlet, "to how many the knowledge of the intended effort was communicated, who without signifying their assent, or attending any of the meetings, were yet prepared to profit by events. That there are many who would not have permitted the enterprise to have failed at a critical moment, for the want of their co-operation, we have the best reason for believing." So believed the community at large; and the panic was in proportion, when the whole danger was finally made public. "The scenes I witnessed," says one who has since narrated the circumstances, "and the declaration of the impending danger that met us at all times and on all occasions, forced the conviction that never were an entire people more thoroughly alarmed than were the people of Charleston at that time. . . . During the excitement, and the trial of the supposed conspirators, rumor proclaimed all, and doubtless more than all, the horrors of the plot. The

city was to be fired in every quarter; the
arsenal in the immediate vicinity was to be
broken open, and the arms distributed to the
insurgents, and a universal massacre of the
white inhabitants to take place. Nor did there
seem to be any doubt in the mind of the people,
that such would actually have been the result
had not the plot fortunately been detected
before the time appointed for the outbreak. It
was believed, as a matter of course, that every
black in the city would join in the insurrection,
and that if the original design had been
attempted, and the city taken by surprise, the
negroes would have achieved a complete and
easy victory. Nor does it seem at all impossible that such might have been, or yet may
be, the case, if any well-arranged and resolute
rising should take place."

Indeed, this universal admission, that all the
slaves were ready to take part in any desperate
enterprise, was one of the most startling aspects
of the affair. The authorities say that the two
principal State's evidence declared that "they
never spoke to any person of color on the

subject, or knew of any one who had been
spoken to by the other leaders, who had withheld his assent." And the conspirators seem
to have been perfectly satisfied that all the
remaining slaves would enter their ranks upon
the slightest success. "Let us assemble a
sufficient number to commence the work with
spirit, and we'll not want men; they'll fall in
behind us fast enough." And as an illustration
of this readiness, the official report mentions
a slave who had belonged to one master for
sixteen years, sustaining a high character for
fidelity and affection, who had twice travelled
with him through the Northern States, resisting
every solicitation to escape, and who yet was
very deeply concerned in the insurrection,
though knowing it to involve the probable
destruction of the whole family with whom he
lived.

One singular circumstance followed the first
rumors of the plot. Several white men, said to
be of low and unprincipled character, at once
began to make interest with the supposed
leaders among the slaves, either from genuine

sympathy, or with the intention of betraying them for money, or by profiting by the insurrection, should it succeed. Four of these were brought to trial; but the official report expresses the opinion that many more might have been discovered but for the inadmissibility of slave testimony against whites. Indeed, the evidence against even these four was insufficient for a capital conviction, although one was overheard, through stratagem, by the intendant himself, and arrested on the spot. This man was a Scotchman, another a Spaniard, a third a German, and the fourth a Carolinian. The last had for thirty years kept a shop in the neighborhood of Charleston; he was proved to have asserted that " the negroes had as much right to fight for their liberty as the white people," had offered to head them in the enterprise, and had said that in three weeks he would have two thousand men. But in no case, it appears, did these men obtain the confidence of the slaves; and the whole plot was conceived and organized, so far as appears, without the slightest co-operation from any white man.

The trial of the conspirators began on Wednesday, June 19. At the request of the intendant, Justices Kennedy and Parker summoned five freeholders (Messrs. Drayton, Heyward, Pringle, Legaré, and Turnbull) to constitute a court, under the provisions of the Act "for the better ordering and governing negroes and other slaves." The intendant laid the case before them, with a list of prisoners and witnesses. By a vote of the court, all spectators were excluded, except the owners and counsel of the slaves concerned. No other colored person was allowed to enter the jail, and a strong guard of soldiers was kept always on duty around the building. Under these general arrangements the trials proceeded with elaborate formality, though with some variations from ordinary usage, — as was, indeed, required by the statute.

For instance, the law provided that the testimony of any Indian or slave could be received, without oath, against a slave or free colored person, although it was not valid, even under oath, against a white. But it is best to

quote the official language in respect to the
rules adopted: "As the court had been organized under a statute of a peculiar and local
character, and intended for the government of
a distinct class of persons in the community,
they were bound to conform their proceedings
to its provisions, which depart in many essential
features from the principles of the common
law and some of the settled rules of evidence.
The court, however, determined to adopt those
rules, whenever they were not repugnant to nor
expressly excepted by that statute, nor incon-
sistent with the local situation and policy of the
State; and laid down for their own government
the following regulations: First, that no slave
should be tried except in the presence of his
owner or his counsel, and that notice should be
given in every case at least one day before the
trial; second, that the testimony of one witness,
unsupported by additional evidence or by circumstances, should lead to no conviction of a
capital nature; third, that the witnesses should
be confronted with the accused and with each
other in every case, except where testimony

was given under a solemn pledge that the
names of the witnesses should not be divulged,
— as they declared, in some instances, that they
apprehended being murdered by the blacks, if
it was known that they had volunteered their
evidence; fourth, that the prisoners might be
represented by counsel, whenever this was
requested by the owners of the slaves, or by
the prisoners themselves if free; fifth, that the
statements or defences of the accused should
be heard in every case, and they be permitted
themselves to examine any witness they thought
proper."

It is singular to observe how entirely these
rules seem to concede that a slave's life has no
sort of value to himself, but only to his master.
His master, not he himself, must choose whether
it be worth while to employ counsel. His
master, not his mother or his wife, must be
present at the trial. So far is this carried, that
the provision to exclude " persons who had no
particular interest in the slaves accused " seems
to have excluded every acknowledged relative
they had in the world, and admitted only those

who had invested in them so many dollars.
And yet the very first section of that part of
the statute under which they were tried lays
down an explicit recognition of their humanity: "And whereas natural justice forbids that
any *person*, of what condition soever, should be
condemned unheard." So thoroughly, in the
whole report, are the ideas of person and
chattel intermingled, that when Gov. Bennett
petitions for mitigation of sentence in the case
of his slave Batteau, and closes, "I ask this,
gentlemen, as an individual incurring a severe
and distressing loss," it is really impossible to
decide whether the predominant emotion be
affectional or financial.

It is a matter of painful necessity to acknowledge that the proceedings of most slave-
tribunals have justified the honest admission of
Gov. Adams of South Carolina, in his legisla-
tive message of 1855: "The administration
of our laws, in relation to our colored population, by our courts of magistrates and freeholders, as these courts are at present constituted,
calls loudly for reform. Their decisions are

rarely in conformity with justice or humanity." This trial, as reported by the justices themselves, seems to have been no worse than the average, — perhaps better. In all, thirty-five were sentenced to death, thirty-four to transportation, twenty-seven acquitted by the court, and twenty-five discharged without trial, by the Committee of Vigilance, — making in all one hundred and twenty-one.

The sentences pronounced by Judge Kennedy upon the leading rebels, while paying a high tribute to their previous character, of course bring all law and all Scripture to prove the magnitude of their crime. "It is a melancholy fact," he says, "that those servants in whom we reposed the most unlimited confidence have been the principal actors in this wicked scheme." Then he rises into earnest appeals. "Are you incapable of the heavenly influence of that gospel, all whose paths are peace? It was to reconcile us to our destiny on earth, and to enable us to discharge with fidelity all our duties, whether as master or servant, that those inspired precepts were imparted by Heaven to fallen man."

To these reasonings the prisoners had, of course, nothing to say; but the official reports bear the strongest testimony to their fortitude. "Rolla, when arraigned, affected not to understand the charge against him, and, when it was at his request further explained to him, assumed, with wonderful adroitness, astonishment and surprise. He was remarkable, throughout his trial, for great presence and composure of mind. When he was informed he was convicted, and was advised to prepare for death, though he had previously (but after his trial) confessed his guilt, he appeared perfectly confounded, but exhibited no signs of fear. In Ned's behavior there was nothing remarkable; but his countenance was stern and immovable, even whilst he was receiving the sentence of death: from his looks it was impossible to discover or conjecture what were his feelings. Not so with Peter: for in his countenance were strongly marked disappointed ambition, revenge, indignation, and an anxiety to know how far the discoveries had extended; and the same emotions were exhibited in his conduct. He did not appear to fear personal consequences, for his whole behavior indicated the reverse; but exhibited an evident anxiety for the success of their plan, in which his whole soul was embarked. His countenance and behavior were the same when he received his sentence; and his only words were, on retiring, 'I suppose you'll let me see my wife and family before I die?' and that not in a supplicating tone. When he was asked, a day or two after, if it was possible he could wish to see his master and family murdered, who had treated him so kindly, he only replied to the question by a smile. Monday's behavior was not peculiar. When he was before the court, his arms were folded; he heard the testimony given against him, and received his sentence, with the utmost firmness and composure. But no description can accurately convey to others the impression which the trial, defence, and appearance of Gullah Jack made on those who witnessed the workings of his cunning and rude address. When arrested and brought before the court, in company with another African named Jack, the property of the estate of Pritchard, he assumed so much ignorance, and looked and acted the fool so well, that some of the court could not believe that this was the necromancer who was sought after. This conduct he continued when on his trial, until he saw the witnesses and heard the testimony as it progressed against him; when, in an instant, his countenance was lighted up as if by lightning, and his wildness and vehemence of gesture, and the malignant glance with which he eyed the witnesses who appeared against him, all indicated the savage, who indeed had been *caught*, but not *tamed*. His courage, however, soon forsook him. When he received sentence of death, he earnestly implored that a fortnight longer might be allowed him, and then a week longer, which he continued earnestly to solicit until he was taken from the court-room to his cell; and when he was carried to execution, he gave up his spirit without firmness or composure."

Not so with Denmark Vesey. The plans of years were frustrated; his own life and liberty were thrown away; many others were sacri-

ficed through his leadership; and one more was
added to the list of unsuccessful insurrections.
All these disastrous certainties he faced calmly,
and gave his whole mind composedly to the
conducting of his defence. With his arms
tightly folded, and his eyes fixed on the floor,
he attentively followed every item of the testimony. He heard the witnesses examined by
the court, and cross-examined by his own
counsel; and it is evident from the narrative of
the presiding judge, that he showed no small
skill and policy in the searching cross-examina-
tion which he then applied. The fears, the
feelings, the consciences, of those who had betrayed him, all were in turn appealed to; but
the facts were quite overpowering, and it was
too late to aid his comrades or himself. Then
turning to the court, he skilfully availed himself of the point which had so much impressed
the community : the intrinsic improbability that
a man in his position of freedom and prosperity
should sacrifice every thing to free other people.
If they thought it so incredible, why not give
him the benefit of the incredibility? The act

being, as they stated, one of infatuation, why convict him of it on the bare word of men who, by their own showing, had not only shared the infatuation, but proved traitors to it? An ingenious defence, — indeed, the only one which could by any possibility be suggested, anterior to the days of Choate and somnambulism; but in vain. He was sentenced; and it was not, apparently, till the judge reproached him for the destruction he had brought on his followers, that he showed any sign of emotion. Then the tears came into his eyes. But he said not another word.

The executions took place on five different days; and, bad as they were, they might have been worse. After the imaginary Negro Plot of New York, in 1741, thirteen negroes had been judicially burned alive; two had suffered the same sentence at Charleston in 1808; and it was undoubtedly some mark of progress, that in this case the gallows took the place of the flames. Six were hanged on July 2, upon Blake's lands, near Charleston, — Denmark Vesey, Peter Poyas, Jesse, Ned, Rolla, and

Batteau, — the last three being slaves of the
governor himself. Gullah Jack and John were
executed "on the Lines," near Charleston, on
July 12; and twenty-two more on July 26.
Four others suffered their fate on July 30; and
one more, William Garner, effected a temporary escape, was captured, and tried by a different court, and was finally executed on
Aug. 9.

  The self-control of these men did not desert
them at their execution. When the six leaders
suffered death, the report says, Peter Poyas
repeated his charge of secrecy : "Do not open
your lips ; die silent, as you shall see me do ; "
and all obeyed. And though afterwards, as
the particulars of the plot became better known,
there was less inducement to conceal, yet every
one of the thirty-five seems to have met his
fate bravely, except the conjurer. Gov. Bennett, in his letter, expresses much dissatisfac-
tion at the small amount learned from the
participators. "To the last hour of the existence of several who appeared to be conspicuous
actors in the drama, they were pressingly im-

portuned to make further confessions," — this "importuning" being more clearly defined in a letter of Mr. Ferguson, owner of two of the slaves, as "having them severely corrected." Yet so little was obtained, that the governor was compelled to admit at last that the really essential features of the plot were not known to any of the informers.

It is to be remembered, that the plot failed because a man unauthorized and incompetent, William Paul, undertook to make enlistments on his own account. He happened on one of precisely that class of men, — favored house-servants, — whom his leaders had expressly reserved for more skilful manipulations. He being thus detected, one would have supposed that the discovery of many accomplices would at once have followed. The number enlisted was counted by thousands; yet for twenty-nine days after the first treachery, and during twenty days of official examination, only fifteen of the conspirators were ferreted out. Meanwhile the informers' names had to be concealed with the utmost secrecy; they were in peril of

their lives from the slaves, — William Paul
scarcely dared to go beyond the doorstep, —
and the names of important witnesses examined
in June were still suppressed in the official
report published in October. That a conspiracy on so large a scale should have existed in
embryo during four years, and in an active
form for several months, and yet have been so
well managed, that, after actual betrayal, the
authorities were again thrown off their guard,
and the plot nearly brought to a head again, —
this certainly shows extraordinary ability in
the leaders, and a talent for concerted action
on the part of slaves generally, with which they
have hardly been credited.

And it is also to be noted, that the range of
the conspiracy extended far beyond Charleston.
It was proved that Frank, slave of Mr. Ferguson, living nearly forty miles from the city, had
boasted of having enlisted four plantations in
his immediate neighborhood. It was in evidence that the insurgents " were trying all
round the country, from Georgetown and Santee round about to Combahee, to get people ; "

and, after the trials, it was satisfactorily established that Vesey " had been in the country as far north as South Santee, and southwardly as far as the Euhaws, which is between seventy and eighty miles from the city." Mr. Ferguson himself testified that the good order of any gang was no evidence of their ignorance of the plot, since the behavior of his own initiated slaves had been unexceptionable, in accordance with Vesey's directions.

With such an organization and such materials, there was nothing in the plan which could be pronounced incredible or impracticable. There is no reason why they should not have taken the city. After all the governor's entreaties as to moderate language, the authorities were obliged to admit that South Carolina had been saved from a " horrible catastrophe." " For, although success could not possibly have attended the conspirators, yet, before their suppression, Charleston would probably have been wrapped in flames, many valuable lives would have been sacrificed, and an immense loss of property sustained by the

citizens, even though no other distressing occur-
rences were experienced by them; while the
plantations in the lower country would have
been disorganized, and the agricultural interests have sustained an enormous loss." The
Northern journals had already expressed still
greater anxieties. "It appears," said the New-
York *Commercial Advertiser*, "that, but for the
timely disclosure, the whole of that State would
in a few days have witnessed the horrid spec-
tacle once witnessed in St. Domingo."

My friend, David Lee Child, has kindly communicated to me a few memoranda of a conversation held long since with a free colored man
who had worked in Vesey's shop during the
time of the insurrection; and these generally
confirm the official narratives. "I was a young
man then," he said; "and, owing to the policy of preventing communication between free
colored people and slaves, I had little opportunity of ascertaining how the slaves felt about
it. I know that several of them were abused
in the street, and some put in prison, for
appearing in sackcloth. There was an ordi-

nance of the city, that any slave who wore a
badge of mourning should be imprisoned and
flogged. They generally got the law, which is
thirty-nine lashes ; but sometimes it was according to the decision of the court." " I heard,
at the time, of arms being buried in coffins at
Sullivan's Island." " In the time of the insurrection, the slaves were tried in a small room
in the jail where they were confined. No
colored person was allowed to go within two
squares of the prison. Those two squares were
filled with troops, five thousand of whom were
on duty day and night. I was told, Vesey said
to those that tried him, that the work of insurrection would go on ; but as none but white
persons were permitted to be present, I cannot
tell whether he said it."

During all this time there was naturally
a silence in the Charleston journals, which
strongly contrasts with the extreme publicity
at last given to the testimony. Even the
National Intelligencer, at Washington, passed
lightly over the affair, and deprecated the publication of particulars. The Northern editors,

on the other hand, eager for items, were constantly complaining of this reserve, and calling for further intelligence. "The Charleston
papers," said the Hartford *Courant* of July
16, "have been silent on the subject of the
insurrection; but letters from this city state
that it has created much alarm, and that two
brigades of troops were under arms for some
time to suppress any risings that might have
taken place." "You will doubtless hear,"
wrote a Charleston correspondent of the same
paper, just before, "many reports, and some
exaggerated ones." "There was certainly a
disposition to revolt, and some preparations
made, principally by the plantation negroes, to
take the city." "We hoped they would progress so far as to enable us to ascertain and
punish the ringleaders." "Assure my friends
that we feel in perfect security, although the
number of nightly guards, and other demon-
strations, may induce a belief among strangers
to the contrary."

The strangers would have been very blind
strangers, if they had not been more influenced

by the actions of the Charleston citizens than
by their words. The original information was
given on May 25, 1822. The time passed, and
the plot failed on June 16. A plan for its
revival on July 2 proved abortive. Yet a letter
from Charleston, in the Hartford *Courant* of
Aug. 6, represented the panic as unabated:
" Great preparations are making, and all the
military are put in preparation to guard
against any attempt of the same kind again;
but we have no apprehension of its being
repeated." On Aug. 10, Gov. Bennett wrote
the letter already mentioned, which was printed
and distributed as a circular, its object being to
deprecate undue alarm. " Every individual in
the State is interested, whether in regard to his
own property, or the reputation of the State,
in giving no more importance to the transac-
tion than it justly merits." Yet, five days after
this, — two months after the first danger had
passed, — a re-enforcement of United-States
troops arrived at Fort Moultrie; and, during
the same month, several different attempts were
made by small parties of armed negroes to cap-

ture the mails between Charleston and Savannah, and a reward of two hundred dollars was offered for their detection.

The first official report of the trials was prepared by the intendant, by request of the city council. It passed through four editions in a few months, — the first and fourth being published in Charleston, and the second and third in Boston. Being, however, but a brief pamphlet, it did not satisfy the public curiosity; and in October of the same year (1822), a larger volume appeared at Charleston, edited by the magistrates who presided at the trials, — Lionel H. Kennedy and Thomas Parker. It contains the evidence in full, and a separate narrative of the whole affair, more candid and lucid than any other which I have found in the newspapers or pamphlets of the day. It exhibits that rarest of all qualities in a slave-community, a willingness to look facts in the face. This narrative has been faithfully followed, with the aid of such cross-lights as could be secured from many other quarters, in preparing the present history.

The editor of the first official report racked

his brains to discover the special causes of the
revolt, and never trusted himself to allude to
the general one. The negroes rebelled because
they were deluded by Congressional eloquence;
or because they were excited by a church squab-
ble; or because they had been spoilt by mistaken indulgences, such as being allowed to
learn to read, — " a misguided benevolence,"
as he pronounces it. So the Baptist Convention seems to have thought it was because
they were not Baptists; and an Episcopal pam-
phleteer, because they were not Episcopalians.
It never seems to occur to any of these spectators, that these people rebelled simply because
they were slaves, and wished to be free.

No doubt, there were enough special torches
with which a man so skilful as Denmark Vesey
could kindle up these dusky powder-magazines;
but, after all, the permanent peril lay in the
powder. So long as that existed, every thing
was incendiary. Any torn scrap in the street
might contain a Missouri-Compromise speech,
or a report of the last battle in St. Domingo,
or one of those able letters of Boyer's which

were winning the praise of all, or one of John
Randolph's stirring speeches in England against
the slave-trade. The very newspapers which
reported the happy extinction of the insurrection by the hanging of the last conspirator,
William Garner, reported also, with enthusi-
astic indignation, the massacre of the Greeks
at Constantinople and at Scio ; and then the
Northern editors, breaking from their usual
reticence, pointed out the inconsistency of
Southern journals in printing, side by side,
denunciations of Mohammedan slave-sales, and
advertisements of those of Christians.

Of course the insurrection threw the whole
slavery question open to the public. "We are
sorry to see," said the *National Intelligencer*
of Aug. 31, "that a discussion of the hateful
Missouri question is likely to be revived, in
consequence of the allusions to its supposed
effect in producing the late servile insurrection
in South Carolina." A member of the Board
of Public Works of South Carolina published
in the Baltimore *American Farmer* an essay
urging the encouragement of white laborers,

and hinting at the ultimate abolition of slavery
"if it should ever be thought desirable." More
boldly still, a pamphlet appeared in Charleston,
under the signature of "Achates," arguing with
remarkable sagacity and force against the whole
system of slave-labor *in towns;* and proposing
that all slaves in Charleston should be sold or
transferred to the plantations, and their places
supplied by white labor. It is interesting to
find many of the facts and arguments of Help-
er's "Impending Crisis" anticipated in this
courageous tract, written under the pressure
of a crisis which had just been so narrowly
evaded. The author is described in the preface
as "a soldier and patriot of the Revolution,
whose name, did we feel ourselves at liberty to
use it, would stamp a peculiar weight and value
on his opinions." It was commonly attributed
to Gen. Thomas Pinckney.

Another pamphlet of the period, also published in Charleston, recommended as a practical
cure for insurrection the copious administration
of Episcopal-Church services, and the prohibition of negroes from attending Fourth-of-July

celebrations. On this last point it is more consistent than most pro-slavery arguments. "The celebration of the Fourth of July belongs *exclusively* to the white population of the United States. The American Revolution was *a family quarrel among equals.* In this the negroes had no concern; their condition remained, and must remain, unchanged. They have no more to do with the celebration of that day than with the landing of the Pilgrims on the rock at Plymouth. It therefore seems to me improper to allow these people to be present on these occasions. In our speeches and orations, much, and sometimes more than is politically necessary, is said about personal liberty, which negro auditors know not how to apply except by running the parallel with their own condition. They therefore imbibe false notions of their own personal rights, and give reality in their minds to what has no real existence. The peculiar state of our community must be steadily kept in view. This, I am gratified to learn, will in some measure be promoted by the institution of the South Carolina Association."

On the other hand, more stringent laws
became obviously necessary to keep down the
advancing intelligence of the Charleston slaves.
Dangerous knowledge must be excluded from
without and from within. For the first purpose
the South Carolina Legislature passed, in December, 1822, the Act for the imprisonment of
Northern colored seamen, which afterwards
produced so much excitement. For the second
object, the Grand Jury, about the same time,
presented as a grievance "the number of
schools which are kept within the city by persons of color," and proposed their prohibition.
This was the encouragement given to the intellectual progress of the slaves; while, as a
reward for betraying them, Pensil, the free
colored man who advised with Devany, received
a present of one thousand dollars; and Devany
himself had what was rightly judged to be the
higher gift of freedom, and was established in
business, with liberal means, as a drayman. He
lived long in Charleston, thriving greatly in his
vocation, and, according to the newspapers,
enjoyed the privilege of being the only man

of property in the State whom a special statute
exempted from taxation.

More than half a century has passed since
the incidents of this true story closed. It has
not vanished from the memories of South Caro-
linians, though the printed pages which once
told it have gradually disappeared from sight.
The intense avidity which at first grasped at
every incident of the great insurrectionary
plot was succeeded by a prolonged distaste for
the memory of the tale; and the official reports
which told what slaves had once planned and
dared have now come to be among the rarest of
American historical documents. In 1841, a
friend of the writer, then visiting South Carolina, heard from her hostess, for the first time,
the events which are recounted here. On
asking to see the reports of the trials, she was
cautiously told that the only copy in the house,
after being carefully kept for years under lock
and key, had been burnt at last, lest it should
reach the dangerous eyes of the slaves. The
same thing had happened, it was added, in many
other families. This partially accounts for the

great difficulty now to be found in obtaining a single copy of either publication; and this is why, to the readers of American history, Denmark Vesey and Peter Poyas have commonly been but the shadows of names.

NAT TURNER'S INSURRECTION

DURING the year 1831, up to the 23d of August, the Virginia newspapers seem to have been absorbed in the momentous problems which then occupied the minds of intelligent American citizens: What Gen. Jackson should do with the scolds, and what with the disreputables? should South Carolina be allowed to nullify? and would the wives of cabinet ministers call on Mrs. Eaton? It is an unfailing opiate to turn over the drowsy files of the Richmond *Enquirer*, until the moment when those dry and dusty pages are suddenly kindled into flame by the torch of Nat Turner. Then the terror flared on increasing, until the remotest Southern States were found shuddering at nightly rumors of insurrection; until far-off European colonies — Antigua, Martinique, Caraccas, Tortola — recognized by some secret

sympathy the same epidemic alarms ; until the
very boldest words of freedom were reported
as uttered in the Virginia House of Delegates
with unclosed doors; until an obscure young
man named Garrison was indicted at common
law in North Carolina, and had a price set
upon his head by the Legislature of Georgia.

Near the south-eastern border of Virginia, in
Southampton County, there is a neighborhood
known as "The Cross Keys." It lies fifteen
miles from Jerusalem, the county - town, or
"court-house," seventy miles from Norfolk, and
about as far from Richmond. It is some ten or
fifteen miles from Murfreesborough in North
Carolina, and about twenty-five from the Great
Dismal Swamp. Up to Sunday, the 21st of
August, 1831, there was nothing to distinguish
it from any other rural, lethargic, slipshod Virginia neighborhood, with the due allotment of
mansion-houses and log huts, tobacco-fields and
"old-fields," horses, dogs, negroes, "poor white
folks," so called, and other white folks, poor
without being called so. One of these last was
Joseph Travis, who had recently married the

widow of one Putnam Moore, and had unfortunately wedded to himself her negroes also.

In the woods on the plantation of Joseph Travis, upon the Sunday just named, six slaves met at noon for what is called in the Northern States a picnic, and in the Southern a barbecue. The bill of fare was to be simple : one brought a pig, and another some brandy, giving to the meeting an aspect so cheaply convivial that no one would have imagined it to be the final consummation of a conspiracy which had been for six months in preparation. In this plot four of the men had been already initiated, — Henry, Hark or Hercules, Nelson, and Sam. Two others were novices, Will and Jack by name. The party had remained together from twelve to three o'clock, when a seventh man joined them, — a short, stout, powerfully built person, of dark mulatto complexion, and strongly marked African features, but with a face full of expression and resolution. This was Nat Turner.

He was at this time nearly thirty-one years old, having been born on the 2d of October,

1800. He had belonged originally to Benjamin Turner, — from whom he took his last name, slaves having usually no patronymic; — had then been transferred to Putnam Moore, and then to his present owner. He had, by his own account, felt himself singled out from childhood for some great work; and he had some peculiar marks on his person, which, joined to his mental precocity, were enough to occasion, among his youthful companions, a superstitious faith in his gifts and destiny. He had some mechanical ingenuity also; experimentalized very early in making paper, gunpowder, pottery, and in other arts, which, in later life, he was found thoroughly to understand. His moral faculties appeared strong, so that white witnesses admitted that he had never been known to swear an oath, to drink a drop of spirits, or to commit a theft. And, in general, so marked were his early peculiarities that people said "he had too much sense to be raised; and, if he was, he would never be of any use as a slave." This impression of personal destiny grew with his growth: he fasted,

prayed, preached, read the Bible, heard voices
when he walked behind his plough, and communicated his revelations to the awe-struck
slaves.   They told him, in return, that, "if
they had his sense, they would not serve any
master in the world."

The biographies of slaves can hardly be indi-
vidualized ; they belong to the class. We know
bare facts ; it is only the general experience
of human beings in like condition which can
clothe them with life. The outlines are certain,
the details are inferential.   Thus, for instance,
we know that Nat Turner's young wife was a
slave ; we know that she belonged to a different
master from himself; we know little more than
this, but this is much.   For this is equivalent
to saying, that, by day or by night, her husband had no more power to protect her than the
man who lies bound upon a plundered vessel's
deck has power to protect his wife on board
the pirate schooner disappearing in the horizon.
She may be well treated, she may be outraged ;
it is in the powerlessness that the agony lies.
There is, indeed, one thing more which we do

know of this young woman: the Virginia newspapers state that she was tortured under the
lash, after her husband's execution, to make
her produce his papers: this is all.

What his private experiences and special
privileges or wrongs may have been, it is
therefore now impossible to say. Travis was
declared to be "more humane and fatherly to
his slaves than any man in the county;" but
it is astonishing how often this phenomenon
occurs in the contemporary annals of slave
insurrections. The chairman of the county
court also stated, in pronouncing sentence, that
Nat Turner had spoken of his master as "only
too indulgent;" but this, for some reason, does
not appear in his printed Confession, which only
says, "He was a kind master, and placed the
greatest confidence in me." It is very possible
that it may have been so, but the printed
accounts of Nat Turner's person look suspicious: he is described in Gov. Floyd's proclamation as having a scar on one of his temples,
also one on the back of his neck, and a large
knot on one of the bones of his right arm,

produced by a blow; and although these were explained away in Virginia newspapers as having been produced by fights with his companions, yet such affrays are entirely foreign to the admitted habits of the man. It must therefore remain an open question, whether the scars and the knot were produced by black hands or by white.

Whatever Nat Turner's experiences of slavery might have been, it is certain that his plans were not suddenly adopted, but that he had brooded over them for years. To this day there are traditions among the Virginia slaves of the keen devices of "Prophet Nat." If he was caught with lime and lampblack in hand, conning over a half-finished county-map on the barn-door, he was always "planning what to do if he were blind;" or, "studying how to get to Mr. Francis's house." When he had called a meeting of slaves, and some poor whites came eavesdropping, the poor whites at once became the subjects for discussion: he incidentally mentioned that the masters had been heard threatening to drive them away; one slave had

been ordered to shoot Mr. Jones's pigs, another
to tear down Mr. Johnson's fences. The poor
whites, Johnson and Jones, ran home to see to
their homesteads, and were better friends than
ever to Prophet Nat.

He never was a Baptist preacher, though
such vocation has often been attributed to him.
The impression arose from his having immersed
himself, during one of his periods of special
enthusiasm, together with a poor white man
named Brantley. "About this time," he says
in his Confession, "I told these things to a
white man, on whom it had a wonderful effect;
and he ceased from his wickedness, and was
attacked immediately with a cutaneous erup-
tion, and the blood oozed from the pores of his
skin, and after praying and fasting nine days
he was healed. And the Spirit appeared to
me again, and said, as the Saviour had been
baptized, so should we be also; and when the
white people would not let us be baptized
by the church, we went down into the water
together, in the sight of many who reviled us,
and were baptized by the Spirit. After this
I rejoiced greatly, and gave thanks to God."

The religious hallucinations narrated in his Confession seem to have been as genuine as the average of such things, and are very well expressed. The account reads quite like Jacob Behmen. He saw white spirits and black spirits contending in the skies; the sun was darkened, the thunder rolled. "And the Holy Ghost was with me, and said, 'Behold me as I stand in the heavens!' And I looked, and saw the forms of men in different attitudes. And there were lights in the sky, to which the children of darkness gave other names than what they really were; for they were the lights of the Saviour's hands, stretched forth from east to west, even as they were extended on the cross on Calvary, for the redemption of sinners." He saw drops of blood on the corn: this was Christ's blood, shed for man. He saw on the leaves in the woods letters and numbers and figures of men, — the same symbols which he had seen in the skies. On May 12, 1828, the Holy Spirit appeared to him, and proclaimed that the yoke of Jesus must fall on him, and he must fight against the serpent when the sign appeared.

Then came an eclipse of the sun in February, 1831: this was the sign; then he must arise and prepare himself, and slay his enemies with their own weapons; then also the seal was removed from his lips, and then he confided his plans to four associates.

When he came, therefore, to the barbecue on the appointed Sunday, and found not these four only, but two others, his first question to the intruders was, how they came thither. To this Will answered manfully, that his life was worth no more than the others, and "his liberty was as dear to him." This admitted him to confidence; and as Jack was known to be entirely under Hark's influence, the strangers were no bar to their discussion. Eleven hours they remained there, in anxious consultation: one can imagine those dusky faces, beneath the funereal woods, and amid the flickering of pine-knot torches, preparing that stern revenge whose shuddering echoes should ring through the land so long. Two things were at last decided: to begin their work that night; and to begin it with a massacre so swift and irresistible as to create in a few days more terror than many battles, and so spare the need of future bloodshed. " It was agreed that we should commence at home on that night, and, until we had armed and equipped ourselves and gained sufficient force, neither age nor sex was to be spared : which was invariably adhered to."

John Brown invaded Virginia with nineteen men, and with the avowed resolution to take no life but in self-defence. Nat Turner attacked Virginia from within, with six men, and with the determination to spare no life until his power was established. John Brown intended to pass rapidly through Virginia, and then retreat to the mountains. Nat Turner intended to " conquer Southampton County as the white men did in the Revolution, and then retreat, if necessary, to the Dismal Swamp." Each plan was deliberately matured ; each was in its way practicable ; but each was defeated by a single false step, as will soon appear.

We must pass over the details of horror, as they occurred during the next twenty-four

hours. Swift and stealthy as Indians, the black
men passed from house to house, — not pausing,
not hesitating, as their terrible work went on.
In one thing they were humaner than Indians,
or than white men fighting against Indians:
there was no gratuitous outrage beyond the
death-blow itself, no insult, no mutilation ; but
in every house they entered, that blow fell on
man, woman, and child, — nothing that had a
white skin was spared. From every house
they took arms and ammunition, and from a
few money. On every plantation they found
recruits : those dusky slaves, so obsequious to
their master the day before, so prompt to sing
and dance before his Northern visitors, were
all swift to transform themselves into fiends
of retribution now ; show them sword or
musket, and they grasped it, though it were
an heirloom from Washington himself. The
troop increased from house to house, — first to
fifteen, then to forty, then to sixty. Some were
armed with muskets, some with axes, some with
scythes   some came on their masters' horses.
As the numbers increased, they could be

divided, and the awful work was carried on
more rapidly still. The plan then was for an
advanced guard of horsemen to approach each
house at a gallop, and surround it till the others
came up. Meanwhile, what agonies of terror
must have taken place within, shared alike by
innocent and by guilty! what memories of
wrongs inflicted on those dusky creatures, by
some, — what innocent participation, by others,
in the penance! The outbreak lasted for but
forty-eight hours; but, during that period, fifty-
five whites were slain, without the loss of a
single slave.

One fear was needless, which to many a husband and father must have intensified the last
struggle. These negroes had been systemati-
cally brutalized from childhood; they had been
allowed no legalized or permanent marriage;
they had beheld around them an habitual
licentiousness, such as can scarcely exist except
under slavery; some of them had seen their
wives and sisters habitually polluted by the
husbands and the brothers of these fair white
women who were now absolutely in their power.

Yet I have looked through the Virginia newspapers of that time in vain for one charge of
an indecent outrage on a woman against these
triumphant and terrible slaves. Wherever they
went, there went death, and that was all. It
is reported by some of the contemporary newspapers, that a portion of this abstinence was
the result of deliberate consultation among
the insurrectionists; that some of them were
resolved on taking the white women for wives,
but were overruled by Nat Turner. If so, he
is the only American slave-leader of whom we
know certainly that he rose above the ordinary
level of slave vengeance; and Mrs. Stowe's
picture of Dred's purposes is then precisely
typical of his: "Whom the Lord saith unto
us, 'Smite,' them will we smite. We will not
torment them with the scourge and fire, nor
defile their women as they have done with ours.
But we will slay them utterly, and consume
them from off the face of the earth."

When the number of adherents had increased
to fifty or sixty, Nat Turner judged it time to
strike at the county-seat, Jerusalem. Thither

a few white fugitives had already fled, and couriers might thence be despatched for aid to Richmond and Petersburg, unless promptly intercepted. Besides, he could there find arms, ammunition, and money; though they had already obtained, it is dubiously reported, from eight hundred to one thousand dollars. On the way it was necessary to pass the plantation of Mr. Parker, three miles from Jerusalem. Some of the men wished to stop here and enlist some of their friends. Nat Turner objected, as the delay might prove dangerous; he yielded at last, and it proved fatal.

He remained at the gate with six or eight men; thirty or forty went to the house, half a mile distant. They remained too long, and he went alone to hasten them. During his absence a party of eighteen white men came up suddenly, dispersing the small guard left at the gate; and when the main body of slaves emerged from the house, they encountered, for the first time, their armed masters. The blacks halted; the whites advanced cautiously within a hundred yards, and fired a volley; on its being returned, they broke into disorder, and hurriedly retreated, leaving some wounded on the ground. The retreating whites were pursued, and were saved only by falling in with another band of fresh men from Jerusalem, with whose aid they turned upon the slaves, who in their turn fell into confusion. Turner, Hark, and about twenty men on horseback retreated in some order; the rest were scattered. The leader still planned to reach Jerusalem by a private way, thus evading pursuit; but at last decided to stop for the night, in the hope of enlisting additional recruits.

During the night the number increased again to forty, and they encamped on Major Ridley's plantation. An alarm took place during the darkness, — whether real or imaginary, does not appear, — and the men became scattered again. Proceeding to make fresh enlistments with the daylight, they were resisted at Dr. Blunt's house, where his slaves, under his orders, fired upon them; and this, with a later attack from a party of white men near Capt. Harris's, so broke up the whole force that they never re-united.

The few who remained together agreed to separate for a few hours to see if any thing could be done to revive the insurrection, and meet again that evening at their original rendezvous. But they never reached it.

Gloomily came Nat Turner at nightfall into those gloomy woods where forty-eight hours before he had revealed the details of his terrible plot to his companions. At the outset all his plans had succeeded; every thing was as he predicted: the slaves had come readily at his call; the masters had proved perfectly defenceless. Had he not been persuaded to pause at Parker's plantation, he would have been master before now of the arms and ammunition at Jerusalem; and with these to aid, and the Dismal Swamp for a refuge, he might have sustained himself indefinitely against his pursuers.

Now the blood was shed, the risk was incurred, his friends were killed or captured, and all for what? Lasting memories of terror, to be sure, for his oppressors; but, on the other hand, hopeless failure for the insurrection, and certain death for him. What a watch he must have kept that night! To that excited imagination, which had always seen spirits in the sky and blood-drops on the corn and hieroglyphic marks on the dry leaves, how full the lonely forest must have been of signs and solemn warnings! Alone with the fox's bark, the rabbit's rustle, and the screech-owl's scream, the self-appointed prophet brooded over his despair. Once creeping to the edge of the wood, he saw men stealthily approach on horseback. He fancied them some of his companions; but before he dared to whisper their ominous names, "Hark" or "Dred," — for the latter was the name, since famous, of one of his more recent recruits, — he saw them to be white men, and shrank back stealthily beneath his covert.

There he waited two days and two nights, — long enough to satisfy himself that no one would rejoin him, and that the insurrection had hopelessly failed. The determined, desperate spirits who had shared his plans were scattered forever, and longer delay would be destruction for him also. He found a spot which he judged safe, dug a hole under a pile of fence-rails in a

field, and lay there for six weeks, only leaving
it for a few moments at midnight to obtain
water from a neighboring spring. Food he had
previously provided, without discovery, from a
house near by.

Meanwhile an unbounded variety of rumors
went flying through the State. The express
which first reached the governor announced
that the militia were retreating before the
slaves. An express to Petersburg further fixed
the number of militia at three hundred, and of
blacks at eight hundred, and invented a convenient shower of rain to explain the dampened
ardor of the whites. Later reports described
the slaves as making three desperate attempts
to cross the bridge over the Nottoway between
Cross Keys and Jerusalem, and stated that the
leader had been shot in the attempt. Other
accounts put the number of negroes at three
hundred, all well mounted and armed, with two
or three white men as leaders. Their intention
was supposed to be to reach the Dismal Swamp,
and they must be hemmed in from that side.

Indeed, the most formidable weapon in the

hands of slave insurgents is always this blind
panic they create, and the wild exaggerations
which follow.   The worst being possible, every
one takes the worst for granted.   Undoubtedly
a dozen armed men could have stifled this
insurrection, even after it had commenced
operations ; but it is the fatal weakness of a
rural slaveholding community, that it can never
furnish men promptly for such a purpose.
" My first intention was," says one of the most
intelligent newspaper narrators of the affair,
" to have attacked them with thirty or forty
men; but those who had families here were
strongly opposed to it."

As usual, each man was pinioned to his own
hearth-stone.   As usual, aid had to be summoned from a distance ; and, as usual, the
United-States troops were the chief reliance.
Col. House, commanding at Fort Monroe, sent
at once three companies of artillery under
Lieut.-Col. Worth, and embarked them on board
the steamer " Hampton " for Suffolk.   These
were joined by detachments from the United-
States ships " Warren " and " Natchez," the

whole amounting to nearly eight hundred men. Two volunteer companies went from Richmond, four from Petersburg, one from Norfolk, one from Portsmouth, and several from North Carolina. The militia of Norfolk, Nansemond, and Princess Anne Counties, and the United-States troops at Old Point Comfort, were ordered to scour the Dismal Swamp, where it was believed that two or three thousand fugitives were preparing to join the insurgents. It was even proposed to send two companies from New York and one from New London to the same point.

When these various forces reached Southampton County, they found all labor paralyzed and whole plantations abandoned. A letter from Jerusalem, dated Aug. 24, says, " The oldest inhabitant of our county has never experienced such a distressing time as we have had since Sunday night last. . . . Every house, room, and corner in this place is full of women and children, driven from home, who had to take the woods until they could get to this place." " For many miles around their track,"

says another "the county is deserted by women
and children." Still another writes, "Jerusalem
is full of women, most of them from the other
side of the river, — about two hundred at
Vix's." Then follow descriptions of the sufferings of these persons, many of whom had lain
night after night in the woods. But the immediate danger was at an end, the short-lived
insurrection was finished, and now the work of
vengeance was to begin. In the frank phrase
of a North-Carolina correspondent, "The
massacre of the whites was over, and the white
people had commenced the destruction of the
negroes, which was continued after our men got
there, from time to time, as they could fall in
with them, all day yesterday." A postscript
adds, that "passengers by the Fayetteville
stage say, that, by the latest accounts, one
hundred and twenty negroes had been killed,"
— this being little more than one day's
work.

These murders were defended as Nat Turner
defended his : a fearful blow must be struck.
In shuddering at the horrors of the insurrection,

we have forgotten the far greater horrors of its suppression.

The newspapers of the day contain many indignant protests against the cruelties which took place. "It is with pain," says a correspondent of the *National Intelligencer*, Sept. 7, 1831, "that we speak of another feature of the Southampton Rebellion; for we have been most unwilling to have our sympathies for the sufferers diminished or affected by their misconduct. We allude to the slaughter of many blacks without trial and under circumstances of great barbarity. . . . We met with an individual of intelligence who told us that he himself had killed between ten and fifteen. . . . We [the Richmond troop] witnessed with surprise the sanguinary temper of the population, who evinced a strong disposition to inflict immediate death on every prisoner."

There is a remarkable official document from Gen. Eppes, the officer in command, to be found in the Richmond *Enquirer* for Sept. 6, 1831. It is an indignant denunciation of precisely these outrages; and though he refuses to give

details, he supplies their place by epithets:
"revolting," — "inhuman and not to be justified," — "acts of barbarity and cruelty," —
"acts of atrocity," — "this course of proceeding
dignifies the rebel and the assassin with the
sanctity of martyrdom." And he ends by
threatening martial law upon all future trans-
gressors. Such general orders are not issued
except in rather extreme cases. And in the
parallel columns of the newspaper the innocent
editor prints equally indignant descriptions of
Russian atrocities in Lithuania, where the Poles
were engaged in active insurrection, amid
profuse sympathy from Virginia.

The truth is, it was a Reign of Terror.
Volunteer patrols rode in all directions, visiting
plantations. "It was with the greatest difficulty," said Gen. Brodnax before the House of
Delegates, "and at the hazard of personal
popularity and esteem, that the coolest and
most judicious among us could exert an influence sufficient to restrain an indiscriminate
slaughter of the blacks who were suspected."
A letter from the Rev. G. W. Powell declares,

"There are thousands of troops searching in every direction, and many negroes are killed every day: the exact number will never be ascertained." Petition after petition was subsequently presented to the Legislature, asking compensation for slaves thus assassinated without trial.

Men were tortured to death, burned, maimed, and subjected to nameless atrocities. The overseers were called on to point out any slaves whom they distrusted, and if any tried to escape they were shot down. Nay, worse than this. "A party of horsemen started from Richmond with the intention of killing every colored person they saw in Southampton County. They stopped opposite the cabin of a free colored man, who was hoeing in his little field. They called out, 'Is this Southampton County?' He replied, 'Yes, sir, you have just crossed the line, by yonder tree.' They shot him dead, and rode on." This is from the narrative of the editor of the Richmond *Whig*, who was then on duty in the militia, and protested manfully against these outrages. "Some of these

scenes," he adds, " are hardly inferior in barbarity to the atrocities of the insurgents."

These were the masters' stories. If even
these conceded so much, it would be interesting
to hear what the slaves had to report. I am
indebted to my honored friend, Lydia Maria
Child, for some vivid recollections of this
terrible period, as noted down from the lips of
an old colored woman, once well known in New
York, Charity Bowery. " At the time of the
old Prophet Nat," she said, " the colored folks
was afraid to pray loud ; for the whites threatened to punish 'em dreadfully, if the least noise
was heard. The patrols was low drunken
whites ; and in Nat's time, if they heard any of
the colored folks praying, or singing a hymn,
they would fall upon 'em and abuse 'em, and
sometimes kill 'em, afore master or missis could
get to 'em. The brightest and best was killed
in Nat's time. The whites always suspect such
ones. They killed a great many at a place
called Duplon. They killed Antonio, a slave
of Mr. J. Stanley, whom they shot ; then they
pointed their guns at him, and told him to

confess about the insurrection. He told 'em he
didn't know any thing about any insurrection.
They shot several balls through him, quartered
him, and put his head on a pole at the fork of
the road leading to the court." (This is no
exaggeration, if the Virginia newspapers may
be taken as evidence.) "It was there but a
short time. He had no trial. They never do.
In Nat's time, the patrols would tie up the free
colored people, flog 'em, and try to make 'em
lie against one another, and often killed them
before anybody could interfere. Mr. James
Cole, high sheriff, said, if any of the patrols
came on his plantation, he would lose his life
in defence of his people. One day he heard a
patroller boasting how many niggers he had
killed. Mr. Cole said, 'If you don't pack up,
as quick as God Almighty will let you, and get
out of this town, and never be seen in it again,
I'll put you where dogs won't bark at you.'
He went off, and wasn't seen in them parts
again."

These outrages were not limited to the
colored population ; but other instances occurred

which strikingly remind one of more recent
times. An Englishman, named Robinson, was
engaged in selling books at Petersburg. An
alarm being given, one night, that five hundred
blacks were marching towards the town, he
stood guard, with others, on the bridge. After
the panic had a little subsided, he happened to
remark, that " the blacks, as men, were entitled
to their freedom, and ought to be emancipated."
This led to great excitement, and he was warned
to leave town. He took passage in the stage,
but the stage was intercepted. He then fled to
a friend's house; the house was broken open,
and he was dragged forth. The civil authorities, being applied to, refused to interfere.
The mob stripped him, gave him a great number of lashes, and sent him on foot, naked,
under a hot sun, to Richmond, whence he with
difficulty found a passage to New York.

Of the capture or escape of most of that
small band who met with Nat Turner in the
woods upon the Travis plantation, little can now
be known. All appear among the list of convicted, except Henry and Will. Gen. Moore,

who occasionally figures as second in command,
in the newspaper narratives of that day, was
probably the Hark or Hercules before mentioned; as no other of the confederates had
belonged to Mrs. Travis, or would have been
likely to bear her previous name of Moore.   As
usual, the newspapers state that most, if not
all the slaves, were "the property of kind and
indulgent masters."

The subordinate insurgents sought safety as
they could.   A free colored man, named Will
Artist, shot himself in the woods, where his
hat was found on a stake and his pistol lying by
him ; another was found drowned ; others were
traced to the Dismal Swamp; others returned
to their homes, and tried to conceal their share
in the insurrection, assuring their masters that
they had been forced, against their will, to join,
— the usual defence in such cases.   The number shot down at random must, by all accounts,
have amounted to many hundreds, but it is past
all human registration now.   The number who
had a formal trial, such as it was, is officially
stated at fifty-five; of these, seventeen were

convicted and hanged, twelve convicted and
transported, twenty acquitted, and four free
colored men sent on for further trial and finally
acquitted. "Not one of those known to be
concerned escaped." Of those executed, one
only was a woman, "Lucy, slave of John T.
Barrow."

There is one touching story, in connection
with these terrible retaliations, which rests on
good authority, that of the Rev. M. B. Cox, a
Liberian missionary, then in Virginia. In the
hunt which followed the massacre, a slaveholder
went into the woods, accompanied by a faithful
slave, who had been the means of saving his
life during the insurrection. When they had
reached a retired place in the forest, the man
handed his gun to his master, informing him
that he could not live a slave any longer, and
requesting him either to free him or shoot him
on the spot. The master took the gun, in some
trepidation, levelled it at the faithful negro, and
shot him through the heart. It is probable that
this slaveholder was a Dr. Blunt, — his being
the only plantation where the slaves were

reported as thus defending their masters. "If
this be true," said the Richmond *Enquirer*,
when it first narrated this instance of loyalty,
"great will be the desert of these noble-minded
Africans."

Meanwhile the panic of the whites continued;
for, though all others might be disposed of, Nat
Turner was still at large. We have positive
evidence of the extent of the alarm, although
great efforts were afterwards made to represent it as a trifling affair. A distinguished
citizen of Virginia wrote, three months later, to
the Hon. W. B. Seabrook of South Carolina,
"From all that has come to my knowledge
during and since that affair, I am convinced
most fully that every black preacher in the
country east of the Blue Ridge was in the
secret." "There is much reason to believe,"
says the Governor's Message on Dec. 6, "that
the spirit of insurrection was not confined to
Southampton. Many convictions have taken
place elsewhere, and some few in distant
counties." The withdrawal of the United-
States troops, after some ten days' service, was

a signal for fresh excitement; and an address, numerously signed, was presented to the United-States Government, imploring their continued stay. More than three weeks after the first alarm, the governor sent a supply of arms into Prince William, Fauquier, and Orange Counties. " From examinations which have taken place in other counties," says one of the best newspaper historians of the affair (in the Richmond *Enquirer* of Sept. 6), " I fear that the scheme embraced a wider sphere than I at first supposed." Nat Turner himself, intentionally or otherwise, increased the confusion by denying all knowledge of the North-Carolina outbreak, and declaring that he had communicated his plans to his four confederates within six months; while, on the other hand, a slave-girl, sixteen or seventeen years old, belonging to Solomon Parker, testified that she had heard the subject discussed for eighteen months, and that at a meeting held during the previous May some eight or ten had joined the plot.

It is astonishing to discover, by laborious comparison of newspaper files, how vast was

the immediate range of these insurrectionary
alarms. Every Southern State seems to have
borne its harvest of terror. On the eastern
shore of Maryland, great alarm was at once
manifested, especially in the neighborhood of
Easton and Snowhill; and the houses of colored
men were searched for arms even in Baltimore.
In Delaware, there were similar rumors through
Sussex and Dover Counties; there were arrests
and executions; and in Somerset County great
public meetings were held, to demand additional
safeguards. On election-day in Seaford, Del.,
some young men, going out to hunt rabbits,
discharged their guns in sport; the men being
absent, all the women in the vicinity took to
flight; the alarm spread like the " Ipswich
Fright "; soon Seaford was thronged with
armed men; and when the boys returned from
hunting, they found cannon drawn out to
receive them.

In North Carolina, Raleigh and Fayetteville
were put under military defence, and women
and children concealed themselves in the
swamps for many days. The rebel organization

was supposed to include two thousand. Forty-six slaves were imprisoned in Union County, twenty-five in Sampson County, and twenty-three at least in Duplin County, some of whom were executed. The panic also extended into Wayne, New Hanover, and Lenoir Counties. Four men were shot without trial in Wilmington, — Nimrod, Abraham, Prince, and " Dan the Drayman," the latter a man of seventy, — and their heads placed on poles at the four corners of the town. Nearly two months afterwards the trials were still continuing; and at a still later day, the governor in his proclamation recommended the formation of companies of volunteers in every county.

In South Carolina, Gen. Hayne issued a proclamation " to prove the groundlessness of the existing alarms," — thus implying that serious alarms existed. In Macon, Ga., the whole population were roused from their beds at midnight by a report of a large force of armed negroes five miles off. In an hour, every woman and child was deposited in the largest building of the town, and a military force

hastily collected in front. The editor of the
Macon *Messenger* excused the poor condition
of his paper, a few days afterwards, by the
absorption of his workmen in patrol duties, and
describes " dismay and terror " as the condition
of the people of "all ages and sexes." In
Jones, Twiggs, and Monroe Counties, the same
alarms were reported; and in one place "several
slaves were tied to a tree, while a militia captain
hacked at them with his sword."

In Alabama, at Columbus and Fort Mitchell,
a rumor was spread of a joint conspiracy of
Indians and negroes. At Claiborne the panic
was still greater: the slaves were said to be
thoroughly organized through that part of the
State, and multitudes were imprisoned; the
whole alarm being apparently founded on one
stray copy of the Boston *Liberator*.

In Tennessee, the Shelbyville *Freeman* announced that an insurrectionary plot had just
been discovered, barely in time for its defeat,
through the treachery of a female slave. In
Louisville, Ky., a similar organization was
discovered or imagined, and arrests were made

in consequence. " The papers, from motives of policy, do not notice the disturbance," wrote one correspondent to the Portland *Courier.* " Pity us ! " he added.

But the greatest bubble burst in Louisiana. Capt. Alexander, an English tourist, arriving in New Orleans at the beginning of September, found the whole city in tumult. Handbills had been issued, appealing to the slaves to rise against their masters, saying that all men were born equal, declaring that Hannibal was a black man, and that they also might have great leaders among them. Twelve hundred stand of weapons were said to have been found in a black man's house ; five hundred citizens were under arms, and four companies of regulars were ordered to the city, whose barracks Alexander himself visited.

If such was the alarm in New Orleans, the story, of course, lost nothing by transmission to other slave States. A rumor reached Frank-fort, Ky., that the slaves already had possession of the coast, both above and below New Orleans. But the most remarkable circum-

stance is, that all this seems to have been a
mere revival of an old terror once before
excited and exploded. The following paragraph
had appeared in the Jacksonville, Ga., *Observer*,
during the spring previous : —

" FEARFUL DISCOVERY. — We were favored, by yesterday's mail, with a letter from New Orleans, of May 1,
in which we find that an important discovery had been
made a few days previous in that city. The following
is an extract: ' Four days ago, as some planters were
digging under ground, they found a square room containing eleven thousand stand of arms and fifteen
thousand cartridges, each of the cartridges containing a
bullet.' It is said the negroes intended to rise as soon
as the sickly season began, and obtain possession of the
city by massacring the white population. The same
letter states that the mayor had prohibited the opening
of Sunday schools for the instruction of blacks, under a
penalty of five hundred dollars for the first offence,
and, for the second, death."

Such were the terrors that came back from
nine other slave States, as the echo of the
voice of Nat Turner. And when it is also
known that the subject was at once taken up
by the legislatures of other States, where there

was no public panic, as in Missouri and Tennessee; and when, finally, it is added that reports of insurrection had been arriving all that year from Rio Janeiro, Martinique, St. Jago, Antigua, Caraccas, and Tortola, — it is easy to see with what prolonged distress the accumulated terror must have weighed down upon Virginia during the two months that Nat Turner lay hid.

True, there were a thousand men in arms in Southampton County, to inspire security. But the blow had been struck by only seven men before; and unless there were an armed guard in every house, who could tell but any house might at any moment be the scene of new horrors? They might kill or imprison negroes by day, but could they resist their avengers by night? "The half cannot be told," wrote a lady from another part of Virginia, at this time, "of the distresses of the people. In South-ampton County, the scene of the insurrection, the distress beggars description. A gentleman who has been there says that even here, where there has been great alarm, we have no idea

of the situation of those in that county. . . .
I do not hesitate to believe that many negroes
around us would join in a massacre as horrible
as that which has taken place, if an opportunity
should offer."

Meanwhile the cause of all this terror was
made the object of desperate search. On Sept.
17 the governor offered a reward of five hundred
dollars for his capture ; and there were other
rewards, swelling the amount to eleven hundred dollars, — but in vain. No one could
track or trap him. On Sept. 30 a minute
account of his capture appeared in the newspapers, but it was wholly false. On Oct. 7
there was another, and on Oct. 18 another ;
yet all without foundation. Worn out by confinement in his little cave, Nat Turner grew
more adventurous, and began to move about
stealthily by night, afraid to speak to any
human being, but hoping to obtain some information that might aid his escape. Returning
regularly to his retreat before daybreak, he
might possibly have continued this mode of
life until pursuit had ceased, had not a dog

succeeded where men had failed. The crea-
ture accidentally smelt out the provisions hid
in the cave, and finally led thither his masters,
two negroes, one of whom was named Nelson.
On discovering the formidable fugitive, they
fled precipitately, when he hastened to retreat
in an opposite direction. This was on Oct. 15;
and from this moment the neighborhood was all
alive with excitement, and five or six hundred
men undertook the pursuit.

It shows a more than Indian adroitness in
Nat Turner to have escaped capture any longer.
The cave, the arms, the provisions, were found;
and, lying among them, the notched stick of
this miserable Robinson Crusoe, marked with
five weary weeks and six days. But the man
was gone. For ten days more he concealed
himself among the wheat-stacks on Mr. Francis's
plantation, and during this time was reduced
almost to despair. Once he decided to surrender himself, and walked by night within
two miles of Jerusalem before his purpose
failed him. Three times he tried to get out
of that neighborhood, but in vain: travelling

by day was of course out of the question, and
by night he found it impossible to elude the
patrol. Again and again, therefore, he returned
to his hiding-place; and, during his whole two
months' liberty, never went five miles from the
Cross Keys. On the 25th of October, he was
at last discovered by Mr. Francis as he was
emerging from a stack. A load of buckshot
was instantly discharged at him, twelve of
which passed through his hat as he fell to the
ground. He escaped even then; but his pursuers were rapidly concentrating upon him, and
it is perfectly astonishing that he could have
eluded them for five days more.

On Sunday, Oct. 30, a man named Benjamin
Phipps, going out for the first time on patrol
duty, was passing at noon a clearing in the
woods where a number of pine-trees had long
since been felled. There was a motion among
their boughs; he stopped to watch it; and
through a gap in the branches he saw, emerging
from a hole in the earth beneath, the face of
Nat Turner. Aiming his gun instantly, Phipps
called on him to surrender. The fugitive,

exhausted with watching and privation, entangled in the branches, armed only with a sword, had nothing to do but to yield, — sagaciously reflecting, also, as he afterwards explained, that the woods were full of armed men, and that he had better trust fortune for some later chance of escape, instead of desperately attempting it then. He was correct in the first impression, since there were fifty armed scouts within a circuit of two miles. His insurrection ended where it began; for this spot was only a mile and a half from the house of Joseph Travis.

Torn, emaciated, ragged, "a mere scarecrow," still wearing the hat perforated with buckshot, with his arms bound to his sides, he was driven before the levelled gun to the nearest house, that of a Mr. Edwards. He was confined there that night; but the news had spread so rapidly that within an hour after his arrival a hundred persons had collected, and the excitement became so intense "that it was with difficulty he could be conveyed alive to Jerusalem." The enthusiasm spread instantly through Virginia; M. Trezvant, the Jerusalem postmaster, sent notices of it far and near; and Gov. Floyd himself wrote a letter to the Richmond *Enquirer* to give official announcement of the momentous capture.

When Nat Turner was asked by Mr. T. R. Gray, the counsel assigned him, whether, although defeated, he still believed in his own Providential mission, he answered, as simply as one who came thirty years after him, " Was not Christ crucified?" In the same spirit, when arraigned before the court, " he answered, ' Not guilty,' saying to his counsel that he did not feel so." But apparently no argument was made in his favor by his counsel, nor were any witnesses called, — he being convicted on the testimony of Levi Waller, and upon his own confession, which was put in by Mr. Gray, and acknowledged by the prisoner before the six justices composing the court, as being " full, free, and voluntary." He was therefore placed in the paradoxical position of conviction by his own confession, under a plea of " Not guilty." The arrest took place on the 30th of October, 1831, the confession on the 1st of November, the trial and conviction on the 5th, and the execution on the following Friday, the 11th of November, precisely at noon.   He met his death with perfect composure, declined addressing the multitude assembled, and told the sheriff in a firm voice that he was ready.   Another account says that he "betrayed no emotion, and even hurried the executioner in the performance of his duty."   "Not a limb nor a muscle was observed to move.   His body, after his death, was given over to the surgeons for dissection."

The confession of the captive was published under authority of Mr. Gray, in a pamphlet, at Baltimore.   Fifty thousand copies of it are said to have been printed; and it was "embellished with an accurate likeness of the brigand, taken by Mr. John Crawley, portrait-painter, and lithographed by Endicott & Swett, at Baltimore."   The newly established *Liberator* said of it, at the time, that it would "only serve to rouse up other leaders, and hasten other insurrections," and advised grand juries to indict Mr. Gray.   I have never seen a copy of the original pamphlet; it is not easily to be found in any of our public libraries; and I have heard of but one as still existing, although the Confession itself has been repeatedly reprinted. Another small pamphlet, containing the main features of the outbreak, was published at New York during the same year, and this is in my possession. But the greater part of the facts which I have given were gleaned from the contemporary newspapers.

Who now shall go back thirty years, and read the heart of this extraordinary man, who, by the admission of his captors, "never was known to swear an oath, or drink a drop of spirits;" who, on the same authority, "for natural intelligence and quickness of apprehension was surpassed by few men," "with a mind capable of attaining any thing;" who knew no book but his Bible, and that by heart; who devoted himself soul and body to the cause of his race, without a trace of personal hope or fear; who laid his plans so shrewdly that they came at last with less warning than any earthquake cn the doomed community around; and who, when that time arrived, took the life of man, woman, and child, without a throb of compunction, a word of exultation, or an act of superfluous outrage? Mrs. Stowe's "Dred" seems dim and melodramatic beside the actual Nat Turner, and De Quincey's "Avenger" is his only parallel in imaginative literature. Mr. Gray, his counsel, rises into a sort of bewildered enthusiasm with the prisoner before him. "I shall not attempt to describe the effect of his narrative, as told and commented on by himself, in the condemned-hole of the prison. The calm, deliberate composure with which he spoke of his late deeds and intentions, the expression of his fiend-like face when excited by enthusiasm, still bearing the stains of the blood of helpless innocence about him, clothed with rags and covered with chains, yet daring to raise his manacled hands to heaven, with a spirit soaring above the attributes of man, — I looked on him, and the blood curdled in my veins."

But, the more remarkable the personal character of Nat Turner, the greater the amazement felt that he should not have appreciated

the extreme felicity of his position as a slave.
In all insurrections, the standing wonder seems
to be that the slaves most trusted and best
used should be most deeply involved. So in
this case, as usual, men resorted to the most
astonishing theories of the origin of the affair.
One attributed it to Free-Masonry, and another
to free whiskey, — liberty appearing dangerous,
even in these forms. The poor whites charged
it upon the free colored people, and urged
their expulsion; forgetting that in North Carolina the plot was betrayed by one of this
class, and that in Virginia there were but two
engaged, both of whom had slave wives. The
slaveholding clergymen traced it¯ to want of
knowledge of the Bible, forgetting that Nat
Turner knew scarcely any thing else. On the
other hand, "a distinguished citizen of Virginia" combined in one sweeping denunciation
"Northern incendiaries, tracts, Sunday schools,
religion, reading, and writing."

But whether the theories of its origin were
wise or foolish, the insurrection made its mark;
and the famous band of Virginia emancipa-

tionists, who all that winter made the House
of Delegates ring with unavailing eloquence, —
till the rise of slave-exportation to new cotton regions stopped their voices, — were but
the unconscious mouthpieces of Nat Turner.
In January, 1832, in reply to a member who
had called the outbreak a "petty affair," the
eloquent James McDowell thus described the
impression it left behind : —

"Now, sir, I ask you, I ask gentlemen in
conscience to say, was that a 'petty affair'
which startled the feelings of your whole population ; which threw a portion of it into alarm,
a portion of it into panic ; which wrung out
from an affrighted people the thrilling cry, day
after day, conveyed to your executive, ' *We are
in peril of our lives ; send us an army for
defence* ' ?   Was that a 'petty affair' which
drove families from their homes, — which
assembled women and children in crowds,
without shelter, at places of common refuge, in
every condition of weakness and infirmity,
under every suffering which want and terror
could inflict, yet willing to endure all, willing

to meet death from famine, death from climate, death from hardships, preferring any thing rather than the horrors of meeting it from a domestic assassin? Was that a 'petty affair' which erected a peaceful and confiding portion of the State into a military camp; which outlawed from pity the unfortunate beings whose brothers had offended; which barred every door, penetrated every bosom with fear or suspicion; which so banished every sense of security from every man's dwelling, that, let but a hoof or horn break upon the silence of the night, and an aching throb would be driven to the heart, the husband would look to his weapon, and the mother would shudder and weep upon her cradle? Was it the fear of Nat Turner, and his deluded, drunken handful of followers, which produced such effects? Was it this that induced distant counties, where the very name of Southampton was strange, to arm and equip for a struggle? No, sir: it was the suspicion eternally attached to the slave himself, — the suspicion that a Nat Turner might be in every family; that the same bloody deed might

be acted over at any time and in any place;
that the materials for it were spread through
the land, and were always ready for a like
explosion. Nothing but the force of this
withering apprehension, — nothing but the
paralyzing and deadening weight with which
it falls upon and prostrates the heart of every
man who has helpless dependants to protect, —
nothing but this could have thrown a brave
people into consternation, or could have made
any portion of this powerful Commonwealth,
for a single instant, to have quailed and
trembled."

While these things were going on, the
enthusiasm for the Polish Revolution was rising
to its height. The nation was ringing with a
peal of joy, on hearing that at Frankfort the
Poles had killed fourteen thousand Russians.
The *Southern Religious Telegraph* was publishing an impassioned address to Kosciuszko;
standards were being consecrated for Poland in
the larger cities; heroes like Skrzynecki,
Czartoryski, Rozyski, Raminski, were choking
the trump of Fame with their complicated

patronymics. These are all forgotten now; and
this poor negro, who did not even possess a
name, beyond one abrupt monosyllable, — for
even the name of Turner was the master's
property, — still lives, a memory of terror, and
a symbol of wild retribution.

APPENDIX OF AUTHORITIES

THE MAROONS OF JAMAICA

1. Dallas, R. C. "The History of the Maroons, from their origin to the establishment of their chief tribe at Sierra Leone: including the expedition to Cuba, for the purpose of procuring Spanish chasseurs; and the state of the Island of Jamaica for the last ten years, with a succinct history of the island previous to that period." In two volumes. London, 1803. [8vo.]

2. Edwards, Bryan. "The History, Civil and Commercial, of the British Colonies in the West Indies. To which is added a general description of the Bahama Islands, by Daniel M'Kinnen, Esq." In four volumes. Philadelphia, 1806. [8vo.]

3. Edwards, Bryan. "Proceedings of the Governor and Associates of Jamaica in regard to the

Maroon Negroes, with an account of the Maroons.''
London, 1796.   8vo.

4. Edwards, Bryan.   '' Historical Survey of St.
Domingo, with an account of the Maroon Negroes,
a history of the war in the West Indies, 1793–94 ''
[etc.].   London, 1801.   4to.

5. *Edinburgh Review*, ii. 376.   [Review of Dallas
and Edwards, by Henry Lord Brougham.]

Also Annual Register, Hansard's Parliamentary
Debates, etc.

[There appeared in *Once a Week* (1865) a paper
entitled '' The Maroons of Jamaica,'' and reprinted
in *Every Saturday* (i. 50, Jan. 31, 1866), in which
Gov. Eyre is quoted as having said, in the London
Times, '' To the fidelity and loyalty of the Maroons
it is due that the negroes did not commit greater
devastation '' in the recent insurrection ; thus curi-
ously repeating the encomium given by Lord Balcarres seventy years before.]

THE MAROONS OF SURINAM

1. '' Narrative of a Five Years' Expedition
against the revolted negroes of Surinam, in Guiana,
on the wild coast of South America, from the year
1772 to 1777 . . . by Capt. J. G. Stedman.''

London.   Printed   for   J.   Johnson,   St.   Paul's Churchyard, and J. Edwards, Pall Mall.   1790. [2 vols. 4to.]

2. "Transatlantic Sketches, comprising visits to the most interesting scenes in North and South America and the West Indies.   With notes on negro slavery and Canadian emigration.   By Capt. J. E. Alexander, 42 Royal Highlanders." London : Richard Bentley, New Burlington St., 1833.   [2 vols. 8vo.]

Also Annual Register, etc.

[The best account of the present condition of the Maroons, or, as they are now called, bush-negroes, of Surinam, is to be found in a graphic narrative of a visit to Dutch Guiana, by W. G. Palgrave, in the *Fortnightly Review*, xxiv. 801 ; xxv. 194, 536.   These papers are reprinted in *Littell's Living Age*, cxxviii. 154, cxxix. 409.   He estimates the present numbers of these people as approaching thirty thousand.   The "Encyclopædia Britannica" gives the names of several publications relating to their peculiar dialect, popularly known as Negro-English, but including many Dutch words.]

GABRIEL'S DEFEAT

The materials for the history of Gabriel's revolt are still very fragmentary, and must be sought in the contemporary newspapers. No continuous file of Southern newspapers for the year 1800 was to be found, when this narrative was written, in any Boston or New-York library, though the Harvard-College Library contained a few numbers of the Baltimore *Telegraphe* and the Norfolk *Epitome of the Times.* My chief reliance has therefore been the Southern correspondence of the Northern newspapers, with the copious extracts there given from Virginian journals. I am chiefly indebted to the Philadelphia *United-States Gazette*, the Boston *Independent Chronicle*, the Salem *Gazette* and *Register*, the New-York *Daily Advertiser*, and the Connecticut *Courant.* The best continuous narratives that I have found are in the *Courant* of Sept. 29, 1800, and the Salem *Gazette* of Oct. 7, 1800; but even these are very incomplete. Several important documents I have been unable to discover, — the official proclamation of the governor, the description of Gabriel's person, and the original confession of the slaves as given to Mr. Sheppard. The discovery of these would no doubt have enlarged, and very probably corrected, my narrative.

DENMARK VESEY

1. " Negro Plot. An Account of the late intended insurrection among a portion of the blacks of the city of Charleston, S.C. Published by the Authority of the Corporation of Charleston." Second edition. Boston : printed and published by Joseph W. Ingraham. 1822. 8vo, pp. 50.

[A third edition was printed at Boston during the same year, a copy of which is in the library of the Massachusetts Historical Society. The first and fourth editions, which were printed at Charleston, S.C., I have never seen.]

2. " An Official Report of the trials of sundry negroes, charged with an attempt to raise an insurrection in the State of South Carolina : preceded by an introduction and narrative ; and in an appendix, a report of the trials of four white persons, on indictments for attempting to excite the slaves to insurrection. Prepared and published at the request of the court. By Lionel H. Kennedy and Thomas Parker, members of the Charleston bar, and the presiding magistrates of the court." Charleston : printed by James R. Schenck, 23 Broad St. 1822. 8vo, pp. 188 x 4.

3. " Reflections occasioned by the late disturb-
ances in Charleston, by Achates."   Charleston:
printed and sold by A. E. Miller, No. 4 Broad St.
1822. 8vo, pp. 30.

4. " A Refutation of the Calumnies circulated
against the Southern and Western States, respect-
ing the institution and existence of slavery among
them.   To which is added a minute and particular
account of the actual state and condition of their
Negro Population, together with Historical Notices
of all the Insurrections that have taken place since
the settlement of the country. — Facts are stubborn
things. — *Shakspeare*.   By a South Carolinian."
[Edwin C. Holland.]   Charleston: printed by
A. E. Miller, No. 4 Broad St.   1822. 8vo, pp. 86.

5. " Rev. Dr. Richard Furman's Exposition of
the views of the Baptists relative to the colored
population in the United States, in a communication to the Governor of South Carolina."   Second
edition.   Charleston: printed by A. E. Miller,
No. 4 Broad St.   1833. 8vo, pp. 16.

[The first edition appeared in 1823.   It relates
to a petition offered by a Baptist Convention for a
day of thanksgiving and humiliation, in reference
to the insurrection, and to a violent hurricane which
had just occurred.]

6. "Practical Considerations, founded on the Scriptures, relative to the Slave Population of South Carolina. Respectfully dedicated to the South Carolina Association. By a South Carolinian." Charleston: printed and sold by A. E. Miller, No. 4 Broad St. 1823. 8vo, pp. 38.

7. [The letter of Gov. Bennett, dated Aug. 10, 1822, was evidently printed originally as a pamphlet or circular, though I have not been able to find it in that form. It may be found reprinted in the *Columbian Centinel* (Aug. 31, 1822), *Connecticut Courant* (Sept. 3), and Worcester *Spy* (Sept. 18). It is also printed in Lundy's *Genius of Universal Emancipation* for September, 1822 (ii. 42), and reviewed in subsequent numbers (pp. 81, 131, 142).]

8. "The Liberty Bell, by Friends of Freedom. Boston: Anti-Slavery Bazaar. 1841. 12mo." [This contains an article on p. 158, entitled "Servile Insurrections," by Edmund Jackson, including brief personal reminiscences of the Charleston insurrection, during which he resided in that city.]

[Of the above-named pamphlets, all now rare, Nos. 1 and 2 are in my own possession. Nos. 3, 4, 5, 6, are in the Wendell Phillips collection of pamphlets in the Boston Public Library.]

NAT TURNER'S INSURRECTION

1. "The Confessions of Nat Turner, the leader
of the late Insurrection in Southampton, Va., as
fully and voluntarily made to Thomas R. Gray, in
the prison where he was confined, and acknowledged by him to be such when read before the
Court of Southampton, with the certificate under
seal of the court convened at Jerusalem, Nov. 5,
1831, for this trial. Also an authentic account of
the whole insurrection, with lists of the whites who
were murdered, and of the negroes brought before
the Court of Southampton, and there sentenced,
etc." New York: printed and published by C.
Brown, 211 Water Street, 1831.

[This pamphlet was reprinted in the *Anglo-
African Magazine* (New York), December, 1859.
Whether it is identical with the work said by the
newspapers of the period to have been published at
Baltimore, I have been unable to ascertain. But
if, as was alleged, forty thousand copies of the
Baltimore pamphlet were issued, it seems impossible that they should have become so scarce. The
first reprint of the Confession, so far as I know,
was a partial one in Abdy's " Journal in the United
States." London. 1835. 3 vols. 8vo.

2. "Authentic and Impartial Narrative of the Tragical Scene which was witnessed in Southhampton County (Va.), on Monday, the 22d of August last, when Fifty-five of its inhabitants (mostly women and children) were inhumanly massacred by the blacks! Communicated by those who were eye-witnesses of the bloody scene, and confirmed by the confessions of several of the Blacks, while under Sentence of Death." [By Samuel Warner, New York.] Printed for Warner & West. 1831. 12mo, pp. 36 [or more, copy incomplete. With a frontispiece]. Among the Wendell Phillips tracts in the Boston Public Library.

3. "Slave Insurrection in 1831, in Southampton County, Va., headed by Nat Turner. Also a conspiracy of slaves in Charleston, S.C., in 1822." New York: compiled and published by Henry Bibb, 9 Spruce St. 1849. 12mo, pp. 12.

[The contemporary newspaper narratives may be found largely quoted in the first volume of the *Liberator* (1831), and in Lundy's *Genius of Universal Emancipation* (September, 1831). The files of the Richmond *Enquirer* have also much information on the subject.]

Other titles of interest

**THE BETRAYAL OF
THE NEGRO
from Rutherford B. Hayes to
Woodrow Wilson**
Rayford W. Logan
New introd. by Eric Foner
459 pp.
80758-0 $15.95

BLACK ABOLITIONISTS
Benjamin Quarles
310 pp.
80425-5 $13.95

**BLACK MAGIC
A Pictorial History of the
African-American in the
Performing Arts**
Langston Hughes and
Milton Meltzer
384 pp., over 400 photos
80406-9 $19.95

BLACK MANHATTAN
James Weldon Johnson
298 pp., 13 illus.
80431-X $14.95

**BLACK MUSICAL THEATRE
From *Coontown* to *Dreamgirls***
Allen Woll
301 pp., 33 illus.
80454-9 $13.95

THE BLACK PANTHERS SPEAK
Edited by Philip S. Foner
Preface by Julian Bond
New foreword by
Clayborne Carson
310 pp., 12 illus.
80627-4 $13.95

**THE BLACK PHALANX
African American Soldiers
in the War of Independence,
the War of 1812, and the
Civil War**
Joseph T. Wilson
New introduction by
Dudley Taylor Cornish
534 pp., 64 illus.
80550-2 $16.95

**THE BOOKS OF AMERICAN
NEGRO SPIRITUALS**
Two volumes in one
J. W. and J. R. Johnson
384 pp.
80074-8 $14.95

**A BRAVE BLACK REGIMENT
The History of the 54th
Massachusetts, 1863–1865**
Captain Luis F. Emilio
New introduction by
Gregory J. W. Urwin
532 pp., 89 photos, 9 maps
80623-1 $15.95

**THE BRIAR PATCH
The Trial of the Panther 21**
Murray Kempton
291 pp.
80799-8 $14.95

**BROWN SUGAR
Eighty Years of America's
Black Female Superstars**
Donald Bogle
208 pp., 183 photos
80380-1 $17.95

**THE COTTON KINGDOM
A Traveller's Observations on
Cotton and Slavery in the
American Slave States**
Frederick Law Olmsted
Edited with an introd.
by Arthur M. Schlesinger
704 pp.
80723-8 $18.95

**ENCYCLOPEDIA OF
BLACK AMERICA**
Edited by W. Augustus Low
and Virgil A. Clift
941 pp., 400 illus.
80221-X $37.50

**FIRE THIS TIME
The Watts Uprising and the 1960s**
Gerald Horne
451 pp., 16 illus., 2 maps
80792-0 $16.95

FREDERICK DOUGLASS
Benjamin Quarles
Introd. by James M. McPherson
408 pp., 9 illus.
80790-4 $15.95

**FREDERICK DOUGLASS ON
WOMEN'S RIGHTS**
Edited by Philip S. Foner
200 pp.
80489-1 $13.95

**JAZZ DANCE
The Story of American
Vernacular Dance**
Marshall and Jean Stearns
New fore- and afterwords by
Brenda Bufalino
506 pp., 32 photos
80553-7 $16.95

LINCOLN AND THE NEGRO
Benjamin Quarles
275 pp., 8 illus.
80447-6 $13.95

**THE MAKING OF AN
AFRO-AMERICAN
Martin Robison Delany**
Dorothy Sterling
368 pp., 3 illus.
80721-1 $14.95

**THE NEGRO IN THE
CIVIL WAR**
Benjamin Quarles
New introduction by
William S. McFeely
402 pp., 4 illus.
80350-X $13.95

**1947: WHEN ALL HELL
BROKE LOOSE IN BASEBALL
The Year Jackie Robinson Broke
the Color Barrier**
Red Barber
380 pp.
80212-0 $14.95